CHICAGO HEIGHTS

CHICAGO HEIGHTS

LITTLE JOE COLLEGE, THE OUTFIT, AND THE FALL OF SAM GIANCANA

CHARLES HAGER WITH DAVID T. MILLER

FOREWORD BY LOUIS CORSINO /
AFTERWORD BY ASHLEIGH D'ANDREA

Southern Illinois University Press / *Carbondale*

Southern Illinois University Press
www.siupress.com

21   20   19   18   4   3   2   1

Publication of this book has been underwritten by the Elmer H.
Johnson and Carol Holmes Johnson criminology fund.

Cover illustration: gun that killed San Giancana (John Binder collection), and approach to Dingess, West Virginia, tunnel (copyright
© 2015 by creator, Prosserman; Creative Commons Attribution
Share Alike 4.0 international license; https://commons.wikimedia.
org/wiki/File:Dingess_Tunnel_Approach.jpg).

Library of Congress Cataloging-in-Publication Data
Names: Hager, Charles, 1950– author. | Miller, David T., author.
Title: Chicago Heights : Little Joe College, the Outfit, and the fall
of Sam Giancana / Charles Hager with David T. Miller; foreword
by Louis Corsino ; afterword by Ashleigh D'Andrea.
Description: Carbondale : Southern Illinois University Press,
[2018] | Includes bibliographical references and index.
Identifiers: LCCN 2017048172 | ISBN 9780809336722 (pbk. : alk.
paper) | ISBN 9780809336739 (e-book)
Subjects: LCSH: Hager, Charles, 1950– | Giancana, Sam,
1908–1975. | Criminals—Illinois—Chicago—Biography. |
Organized crime—Illinois—Chicago. | Mafia—Illinois—Chicago.
Classification: LCC HV6248.H143 A3 2018 | DDC 364.1092 [B]
—dc23 LC record available at https://lccn.loc.gov/2017048172

Printed on recycled paper. ♻

This paper meets the requirements of ANSI/NISO Z39.48 1992
(Permanence of Paper) ∞

To Poppy Claire Hager

To live outside the law, you must be honest.
—*Bob Dylan*

❧ ❧ ❧

CONTENTS

FOREWORD

Traditional organized crime continues to fascinate. Over the past several years a slew of new books has attempted to explain the historical, sociological, and personal situations that led to criminal operations. Indeed, a focus on the Chicago Outfit alone has produced Deirdre Bair's *Al Capone*, John Binder's *Al Capone's Beer Wars*, and my own study *The Neighborhood Outfit: Organized Crime in Chicago Heights*. In their own way and with a less moralistic tone than previous studies, these works provided new insights about the conditions that allowed the Outfit to dominate organized crime in Chicago for the greater part of the past century.

It is in this context that Charles Hager's (with David Miller) *Chicago Heights: Little Joe College, the Outfit, and the Fall of Sam Giancana* enters into and extends the new literature on organized crime and, in particular, the Chicago Outfit. Focused primarily on the Chicago Heights crew, it is a different and provocative book in a number of important ways. First, it examines a component of the Outfit that has received little attention. Though long a major money maker and classic model for running illegal enterprises, the Chicago Heights operation has been largely ignored by scholars, the press, and the public. Hager's work in part remedies this inattention by taking us into the day-to-day workings and criminal activities of the South Side mobsters. Second, it examines these operations at a critical time in the history of the Outfit. Set primarily during the 1960s and early 1970s, this story offers an upfront view of the Outfit as it begins to unravel. We see the Outfit scrambling to make a profit and to recruit new workers. In the process, the mobsters are less glamorous and less romanticized; the criminal operations more random, more mundane. Third, this study draws us in because it is a first-person account of life inside the Outfit from the vantage of a foot soldier. We are given detailed and novel insights on how someone crosses the line and becomes a street-level enforcer and gambling fixer for the Chicago Heights crew. Along the way, we see how Hager is gradually seduced by a life of crime and comes to associate himself with a network of other characters and operatives and learns the ins and outs of stealing cars, running a chop shop, and fixing horse races. It is a coming-of-age story with a twist—a memoir by Hager as he moves from poor farm boy in West Virginia to associate and friend of burglars and hit men in Chicago Heights to young man involved in one of the most notorious and still unsolved crimes in gangland history—the killing of Chicago Outfit leader Sam "Mooney" Giancana.

Indeed, the most compelling aspect of this volume is the manner in which these themes come together in a descriptive account of Giancana's murder. Giancana was killed in the basement of his home in 1975. To this day, attempts to explain this unresolved crime have generated a number of competing explanations. From the facts of the crime and the available evidence, some hold that other Outfit leaders orchestrated the hit because Giancana was scheduled to testify in court and incriminate them. Other explanations suggest that Giancana was long regarded as a liability because he was a bit unstable, a bit "mooney," and was jeopardizing Outfit operations. Some place blame on the Central Intelligence Agency for fears that Giancana would reveal the supposed ties between the Mafia and that organization in the unsuccessful attempt to kill Fidel Castro a number of years previously. All of these explanations are based loosely on the facts of the case, a good deal of supposition, and traditional narratives regarding the conspiratorial adventures of the Mafia and secret government agencies. They may be plausible. Yet there is little evidence or fresh information to support these theories.

Hager's book addresses this problem in some measure by providing a first-person account of Giancana's murder. Specifically, Hager tells of his association with a Chicago Heights hit man who claims to have broken into Giancana's house and shot him in cold blood. We are provided with extensive details and the step-by-step process through which this execution took place. Of course, we are left to wonder whether this account is true, as Hager himself comments. Yet this is where the other major themes of the book make Hager's claim more believable. That is, Hager's gradual development from wide-eyed farm boy to Outfit enforcer in Chicago Heights, which seems plausible given my own research and experiences, adds credibility to his narrative and the willingness of other enforcers and hit men to speak to him about these nefarious dealings. And Hager's more intimate and personal ties with the hit man in question—ties nurtured and graphically described throughout the book—also provide at least circumstantial evidence that the story of Giancana's murder is reasonable. Though we are left with a number of questions and uncertainties, Hager's description is coherent and compelling. The long history and personal circumstances that Hager identifies throughout the book ground Hager's claim that the Giancana murder may have come about in different ways and for different reasons than we have been led to believe.

As I contemplate this work, it is hard not to compare it to some of the well-regarded depictions of organized crime in film and television. *Goodfellas* and *The Sopranos* come to mind. These characterizations had a special appeal because they moved effortlessly between the more prosaic life of gangsters, on the one hand, and the periodic eruption of murder and mayhem on the other. Gangsters are not simply thugs or goons, though they can be, but also people who live normal lives whether that means cooking pasta while trafficking in drugs or taking one's child on a college visit while arranging a hit on a rival gang member. These depictions capture our attention because they convey a reality closer to the truth than more romanticized or moralistic accounts suggest. They also challenge our moral sensibilities, because they blur the line between people and situations we can identify with and criminals and circumstances we find abhorrent. *Chicago Heights: Little Joe College, the Outfit, and the Fall of Sam Giancana* has a similar character. Yet here the places are real, the characters are not actors, and the incidents have true consequences. As such, this work brings us a step closer to understanding the long history of, and our fascination with, organized crime. It helps explain why, despite all the moral implications, organized crime, and depictions of it, will not die.

Louis Corsino
North Central College

CHICAGO HEIGHTS

❧ ❧ ❧

PROLOGUE

On the evening of June 19, 1975, Sam "Momo" Giancana was cooking sausages and peppers in his home in Oak Park, Illinois, a village just west of Chicago, when a gunman shot him in the back of the head, turned his body over, and shot him six more times in the face and neck.[1] His blood had not yet dried before news of the execution of one of America's most recognized crime bosses was splashed over the national press and stayed there for weeks. The story had everything—money, power, sex, crime, politics, and an unsolved murder.

Newspaper readers couldn't get enough as details about Giancana as a mob killer, as a confidante and lover of Marilyn Monroe, and as someone connected to the plans of the Central Intelligence Agency to assassinate Fidel Castro began to dominate the headlines. It would take years for the public to know the reach of his political and social connections, but the gruesome details of his death have become the bloody grist of scores of movies, books, and articles over the ensuing four decades. Every account offers theories about who killed Giancana, and why, but no killer has been charged, much less convicted, and as time has passed the likely culprits have faded into history.

Otherwise, I wouldn't be writing this story, for fear of mob retaliation. But now, more than forty years after the fact, I finally feel safe to tell my story, and with it the story of the Giancana killing. First I need to tell you how I came to be in the Outfit, how I can know what I know. I know about the Giancana killing because I chauffeured the boss who gave the order. I rented my home to the man who pulled the trigger. And I was in the car when Giancana's killer blew off the back of the real killer's head. It took me years to piece it all together, but it fits. And I got the full story of the Giancana hit from the trigger man himself.

This isn't a book about suppositions or theories or conspiracies. What you will read in the following pages is true to the best of my knowledge, and I was there for most of it.

I was born in a squalid hamlet in West Virginia's Hatfield and McCoy hill country, one of ten hungry children who often had nothing more than oatmeal to eat for an entire week. Although I was a ninth grade dropout from an impoverished rural family I was blessed with sharp street smarts, an organized mind, and an unfailing memory. Today, that memory enables me to tell the story of Sam based on events that transpired these decades ago. When I was thirteen my uncle, Columbus Hager, took me out of my rundown Appalachian one-room to Chicago Heights, Illinois, where he ran a bar for the Outfit.[2] Under his tutelage I began my life as a rather naïve apprentice criminal. I moved cars and packages from one place to another, never knowing what was in them, and I was smart enough not to ask. Uncle Columbus never specifically told me, but I realized over time that every car I moved was carrying money or was to be sold or was headed to a chop shop to be stripped of valuable parts.

Coming of age in the Mob in 1960s Chicago was my education not only in the ways of crime but also in the ways of "justice"; during that era the police and courts were almost entirely controlled by organized crime. I rose to become a chauffeur to the top bosses, a fixer of horse races. A bagman for millions of dollars of mob money, and an enforcer of racket collections—the so-called street tax levied by the Outfit. When I discovered how much I loved horses I also became the mob's expert on fixing harness races. Eventually, as I moved up in that world, I became an owner, a trainer, and a driver in that fix-ridden world. I found few things more exciting than putting a pile of money on an array of top trotters running as fast as they could without breaking into a gallop. And I knew how to see to it that the horse I wanted to win did so more often than not.

I was on top of the world. I was young and healthy, I had plenty of money in the bank, I had a family, a successful business, friends who would protect me.

Then one day it all came crashing down.

Five years later I was left with only a prison record and questions that would take me years to answer and would lead to the book you're holding now.

INTRODUCTION

❧ ❧ ❧

The house was dingy, small, run down. I was surprised that a big-deal Chicago hit man who had worked the rackets for years had fallen so far down the ladder. He maneuvered the three steps to the porch with obvious difficulty, paused for a second to get his balance, turned the handle, and pushed open the door. I walked in just behind him and held his arm as he limped toward a chair behind a white kitchen table to the left of the door. He steadied himself with a hand on the table and then flopped into a chair. The meal his long-time girlfriend had fixed for him was still sitting at his place at the table—soup, rolls, and a glass of some drink that I didn't recognize. He told me to sit down, pointing to the chair across from him, but I told him I wanted to stand after my long drive.

The truth was I wanted to have my back against the wall because I didn't know whether anyone else was in the house and I wasn't taking any chances.

Taking a quick look around, with one eye on Duff, I saw that the kitchen walls, floor, and ceiling were painted white, and, as I looked down the hallway, what I could see of the rest of the house appeared to be mostly white also. Duff. His real name was Zazzetti, but I knew him as Duff. I have no idea what other names he used in those years.

Typical of Duff, the kitchen was spotless. He had been in the Army for several years when he was younger, and neatness and order had been drilled into him, along, I guess, with a skill for shooting to kill.

The bare bulb of the kitchen light gave me a better look at him, this hit man and now cancer victim, death waiting behind his dull grey eyes. There was no spark, no animation in him. He was wearing a faded, untucked flowery shirt, and I couldn't tell if he was packing or not. Periodically, he

3

would try to choke down some food, but he soon gagged, spat it out, and pushed the plate back.

"OK, Charley, you went through a lot of trouble with the bosses to force a meet. What's on your mind?"

"What's on my mind?" I thought. "You son of a bitch, you blew the back of my friend's head off right in front of me and landed me in prison for five years, and you wonder what's on my mind?" The rage I'd nursed for five long years in prison rose up in me, and I almost leaped at him to tear his cancer-ridden body apart. But I got myself under control. "I'm here to get answers, and I don't want any crap. I want the truth. Why did you let me rot in a West Virginia prison for a hit I didn't do and didn't even know was going to happen?"

Duff sighed and coughed. "Yeah, I owe you," he said.

"Damn straight," I responded, "Big time." I didn't walk into Bob Duff's house to be jerked around. "Bottom line. Why did you kill Spry? This will be your repayment to me, case closed."

Bob looked up at me with watery eyes, his body and mind weakened by cancer. This wasn't the man I knew five years ago. I had rented my home to him. I pulled his ass out of the trunk of a burning car in a cornfield after he had been robbed, tied up, stabbed, and left to burn. And then I took a murder rap for the son of a bitch. I must be the dumbest man on earth to even be talking to this walking dead man.

But I needed answers from Duff. And now we were alone.

His eyes opened and focused on my face. "OK, Charley. I may not live to see tomorrow, but I owe you this. You did the time for the rap, so here's the truth. Dick Spry cut out on me."

"Cut out on you when? Where?"

"Charley," Duff responded. "This goes to your grave with you, man. Spry ran out on me when we made the hit on Sam." Nothing went to my grave unless I said it did.

I stood still. Sam? My jaws locked and I couldn't speak. Giancana? Damn, I thought, this skeleton in front of me is delusional. He claims he made one of the most famous hits in mob history. I played along.

"Yeah? Tell me."

"OK, but it's complicated, and you gotta swear to take it to the grave with you, Charley. I have family, and I wouldn't want to bring any heat down on them."

Yeah, sure. I responded with the grunt of a half-hearted promise. He reached down, clutching his stomach, and held up a hand. "I gotta have something for the pain, and I need it now. Ya gotta give me a minute."

I had waited this long, so what the hell was a few minutes more? Maybe the painkiller would make it easier for him to talk. There was no doubt he was desperate. Before I could answer he reached across the table and pulled a cardboard box over to him. He clumsily pulled out a small silver teaspoon and set it in front of him, then selected a short candle and a small butane lighter. He lit the candle with a shaking hand. He squirted a syringe of liquid into the bowl of the spoon, added a couple of chunks of brown stuff and put the spoon to one side, then pulled a brown leather strap from the box, wrapped it around his upper arm, and drew it tight. Holding the spoon over the candle with one hand, he picked up another syringe and drew the hot brownish liquid into its barrel. He winced as he stuck the needle in his forearm, just below the elbow, and half-smiled as the heroin hit his bloodstream.

He relaxed and found a new draft of energy.

He sat up and began telling me the story of the hit from the beginning, with clarity and detail. And now, despite my mild vow, I'll tell it to you.

❧ ❧ ❧

BUT FIRST I will tell you how I came to be in the Outfit, on the outskirts of Chicago, in that room, with that dying man.

1. TRIPLY DAMNED

I came into the world on January 12, 1950, wailing bitterly about my unfortunate landing in a dank, sparse, and smelly rural hospital near Dingess, West Virginia. I suspect there was little celebration in the hapless Hager household over one more mouth to feed. Dingess is perched on the northern edge of lands notorious for the four-decade feud between the Hatfields and the McCoys. The impoverished coal country stayed on the sidelines while most of America enjoyed massive social, cultural, technological, and economic advances. Corrupt politics[1] ensured that the educational and infrastructure improvements needed to truly break the poverty chain were supplanted by quick, superficial fixes like food stamps. The cops made certain the town and county were run by cruel, ruthless men, and no sense of justice could ever take hold in a child. As a result, the hill families for miles around the Hager home had been beaten down in body and spirit by too few necessities, too much sickness, and too little hope. I came to life in a region where going to bed hungry and cold was the norm.

The main road into Dingess literally shows off its isolation and darkness, as the traveler must enter the town through an unlit one-lane tunnel nearly a mile long.[2] As I grew I would pass through that tunnel many times, thinking first that the pinpoint of light on the other end was like looking through the wrong end of a telescope. As I grew I would liken leaving Dingess through the tunnel to being born each time, and in a way it was. A new life, a new possibility awaited me on the other side, away from my father and all the turmoil around me. And there would be times when every trip back through it to home felt like dying, the small light at the end telling me to give up as I made my way from the bright lights and excitement of Chicago to the dingy, closed-in Dingess.

Throughout my childhood there was little to eat and much to endure. My mother, who suffered the triple damnation of a drunken husband, a large and growing family, and hopeless poverty, did the very best she could by all of us and continually sacrificed her own needs so that we could survive. The relationship between my much-loved mother and me was as close and protective as it could be. Somewhere among the rare positive thoughts of my dispirited youth I imagine that on that dismal January day of my birth my mother smiled and whispered in my ear, "Hey, little man, this is your mama, and I promise I will always take care of you the best that I can."

I grew up free and wild. When not doing my daily chores, I played all over those West Virginia hills with my brothers and sisters. Our imaginations turned ordinary junk and trash into greater playthings than money could buy. We would be gone from the house for hours, but when the sun went down Mom would step out on the broken-down porch and call us in for supper. It was a race to get to the table because we had been playing all day with nothing to eat since breakfast. If we were lucky, there would be a left-over biscuit for lunch the next day—a rare occurrence in the Hager home.

Most of our sustenance came from the garden or from the kindness of our extended family and neighbors. There was a lot of companionship in this area, and people loved my mother and wanted to help her when they could. Our neighbors knew that it took a heap of food to feed ten hungry kids, and they knew how little we had. When the summer crops came in we ate pretty well from the garden's vegetables and fruit trees. Mom was a woman with strong survival instincts, and she canned as many fruits and vegetables as she could for the harsh winters. I can still see row upon row of shiny Ball jars sitting on a shelf in the kitchen. Those jars looked so good, but we kids knew not to ask her for anything on the shelf because they were there for the dreary winter days that were sure to come. Mom understood the relentless rotation of the seasons and what happened to those who didn't plan ahead as the summer passed by them. A believer in God's word, our mother made sure that we had what we needed before she ever took for herself. Many times after a meal she quietly pushed what was left on her plate to me. She would smile and say, "Son, help me out with this food, I need to keep my girlish figure and simply can't eat another bite."

We lived in a rundown, tarpaper house—real, honest-to-goodness tar-paper. There were cracks between the walls, and in the winter months we often woke to a sprinkle of snow or frost on our bedcovers. In winter and summer alike, the centers of our survival were the massive wood-burning iron cookstove and a potbellied stove for heat. True to the legends of hill-billy living, there was no indoor plumbing in the Hager house. We had an outhouse and bathed in a round tin tub. Of course, going to the outhouse was an ordeal in any weather, but when the winter wind whipped around the corner of the house and there was a foot of snow on the ground, that trip was miserable. The stench would make you hold your breath for as long as you could. Among the daily dilemmas of my youth, one of the most difficult was how long to stay in bed before making a fast walk to the outhouse. I'll admit that I often stained the fresh snow yellow just outside the bleached wooden porch, but I had the sense to kick fresh snow over it so I would not be found out.

The floors in the one-room house were bare, and there were cracks wide enough to let the daylight through to the ground below. Furniture was sparse, but there was a chair for every bottom and a bed for every three or four of us kids. Every night we competed over the blankets and a warm place in the middle of the bed. Strength, size, and age held definite advantages in acquiring and holding this restricted space. The only privacy we had was offered by the outhouse, but the smell was too big a price to pay for anything but the very briefest moment of solitude.

Most mornings my mother would fry fatback bacon in her big iron skillet to get enough grease to make gravy. I can still smell it—and to this day the memory of that bare breakfast repulses me. On good days she would make biscuits and fry potatoes. But it was hard to come up with enough flour to make biscuits for twelve people, and the morning meal was more often plain, unsweetened oatmeal. There were days when even the oatmeal ran out because of Daddy's drinking binges, and we woke up and went to bed hungry.

Our generous Dingess neighbors were attuned to our hardships. Often, at our most desperate times, when our stomachs were empty and the family cupboards stripped bare, there would be a knock on the door and an understanding voice would say, "Just thought you might need. . . ." It was a just-in-time support system that saved us many times with food or hand-me-down clothes. As I grew I recognized more and more clearly that this was not the life I wanted to live; but there was nothing for me to do about it yet.

The Hager shack was twelve miles from the nearest store, and the only way to get there was by foot. That foot was often mine. But more often than not Mom and I walked together to the store and back with the few things we could afford in order to supplement the scant food we had at home. The Dingess country store was a tiny place with only the most basic stock—coffee, tea, flour, sugar, country ham, and eggs. But they did have a pop cooler, and sometimes, though not often, Mom would have an extra dime to buy me a drink. The shelves above the checkout counter were lined with unimaginable wonders like peppermint sticks, gumdrops, and licorice, but all we could do was look at them.

A pointed finger waved under my nose taught me not to touch anything in the store. Once I picked up a tin of Kiwi shoe polish and almost died from embarrassment and shame when a snooty old lady told the clerk that she had better watch me because I was certain to steal that shoe polish. In reality, I was daydreaming about how nice my old shoes would look with a little shine.

I've painted a rural version of Oliver Twist to describe my Appalachian, dirt-road life, but it was not totally lacking special gifts. One of the nicer aspects of life was the sense of community. Neighbors for miles around would share what they had, and that included their horses. A farm about a mile and a half from my home boasted a string of magnificent riding horses, most of which were creamy, elegant Palominos.

But most of the horses in the hills above the tiny Hager farm ran free. You could just pick the one you wanted, jump on its back, and take off like the wind. My favorite riding place was along a shallow mountain creek with a stony bottom and grass-ridged sides. Have you ever seen horses in movies running wild along a shallow creek bed? I can tell you that it feels just as thrilling and fun in reality as it looks on the screen. The feel of that massive beast between your legs and the fast-flying elation of romping bareback down a creek bed is shared by both the horse and rider. All that charging and splashing feels the way real freedom should feel, and it's great fun for a country kid.

A typical day in Dingess would find me up at 5 A.M., helping my mother collect wood to heat water so we could wash our faces and hands. There was a firebox on the side of the cookstove that kept water hot as long as the stove was lit. This old stove allowed Mom to provide heat and hot meals to ten hungry mouths, and she was in that kitchen all day. She washed most of our clothes by hand, stringing a clothesline in the kitchen during the winter months. My mother's hands were always chapped and cracked; gloves and hand lotion were luxuries.

My father's family lost everything they owned during the Great Depression, including a large amount of land with oil, gas, and mineral rights. The coal mining industry, the principal employer in West Virginia, was feast or famine, mainly the latter after the Depression. With neither financial assets nor educational opportunities, many West Virginia families were forced to lease, and then sell, their land in an attempt to start over. Some left the state for Cleveland, Chicago, Baltimore, Detroit, and Phoenix, cities that provided good jobs in manufacturing. People did not want to leave their homes to go elsewhere, but they could not raise their families without the security of a good job.

As I matured and developed some perspective on my life and surroundings, the love of my soft-voiced, raven-haired mother set against the abuse of a drunken, mean-spirited father provided a stark lesson. My mother, Erma Hicks Hager, was beautiful. She had sharp facial features that could make her look stern, but when she smiled it was like the sun came out. She was tall and slender and elegant, with shiny black hair and soft olive skin. She labored in the garden every day of the growing season, washed clothes by hand, carried water and firewood, and took care of her ten children every waking hour.

Mom could afford to buy only two dresses and one pair of shoes every year. She owned one coat. I later wondered how she would look with one of those beauty makeovers, where experts apply magical skills to God-given assets. Humble and full of faith, she was damned to a life with a drunken, deadbeat husband fifteen years her senior.

My father, Robert Hager, was disabled in a logging accident when I was nine years old. Chronic pain contributed to his alcoholism. Dad seemed to make it his mission to foster misery and deprivation in the Hager household. Day after day, year after year, my Mom fed and held the family together on her own, while her shiftless husband inflicted pain and squandered any money or asset we had to feed his overwhelming moonshine habit.

I suppose Dad loved us in his way, but he loved alcohol more. Dingess was home to a thriving moonshine trade. The hooch was brewed by a couple of moonshiners up in the hills, and every holler and hamlet had street sellers who would travel with a horse or donkey up and down the dirt streets, selling pint bottles of grain alcohol. When my father had money for a pint, he'd wait on the porch for the moonshine seller's twice-daily rounds. As the moonshiner approached, Dad would signal and the shiner would come up, collect the price of a pint, tell Dad where the hidden bottle could be found, and be on his way. A bit later, Dad would hobble off on his crutches and retrieve the bottle from a streambed or from under a rock. Most of the time, the bottle was nearly empty before Dad either returned home or fell down to sleep it off. Several times I found him passed out, babbling incoherently to some demon he had seen along the trail back to the house.

Most of the time he drank only when he could scrape up the money, but two or three times a year Dad would go on a binge and be drunk for weeks. He was not a happy drunk. Just the opposite: he was belligerent and at times violent. Every so often Mom would leave Dad. She would take me with her for protection and we would spend time with her parents until he sobered up.

Dad was extremely resentful of my mother. I think that down deep inside he knew that he was letting us down and my mother deserved better. But to feed his alcohol dependency he'd ignore her needs and sell or trade anything of value to buy a bottle of moonshine. When I was seven years old I had a puppy, and he sold it for a bottle of moonshine. My one personal possession, my floppy-eared pal, gone forever because of that selfish drunk. I cried all day. I learned from that experience that you can't trust anyone in this life but yourself and, if you're as lucky as I was, your mother. There were many times when I had to defend her from the demons of alcohol, times when I am sure that my Dad would have killed her in a drunken rage had I not intervened.

I was close to my brother and my sisters. We took care of each other, and we took care of Mom. Della, born one year before me, shared my birthday. When my mother and I went to stay with my grandparents, Della stayed behind to take care of our little brothers and sisters. Della had a way with Dad. She could calm him down most of the time, and when she couldn't, she would take the little kids and hide in the woods until it was safe to return. We were like a tag-team protecting our mother, caring for our younger siblings, and keeping peace in the house. That partnership established a bond that remains today. It's been one of the blessings of my life that our family has remained close.

Neither of my parents could read or write, but Dad chose a path of bitterness and drunkenness to numb the pain of his ignorance, while Mom worked hard, maintained a strong faith, and loved us everlastingly. She sacrificed her very being to see that we were as safe as possible. When I was just ten she learned she had something more than the normal fatigue of a hard-working mother with many children. She had leukemia, at the time a death sentence with only the day and hour unreckoned.

My mother left my dad several times and took us all to stay with her father, but it was a burden on my grandfather to feed and care for so many children. But my mother's father was a kind and giving man and often kept us for several months—no small feat, considering it meant a tableful of hungry kids three times a day. So when Dad eventually sobered up and came around mewling, begging, and promising Mom the world, she would come back home. I later found it odd that my grandfather didn't run my dad off, or worse, but he never did.

Sadly for the Hager kids, the tattered and dingy clothes we wore on the daily bus ride to Dingess Elementary School were a pennant announcing extreme poverty, even among a population that was considered poor by any standard other than rural West Virginia's. While school attire at Dingess Elementary was certainly scruffy, the Hager family presented a new low. Our patched clothes were too big or too small and were faded by countless washings. Our shoes had never seen polish, the heels were worn down, and the toes had tears and holes from growing toes and encounters with bricks and rocks. Two shirts or sweaters were the only winter gear we had, and we stood out among classmates who had coats and hats.

The other kids mocked me, and they angered me. The old yellow school bus was a major source of trouble. The ride to school took more than an hour each way, so it was often still dark when I boarded the bus in the morning and dusk when I returned home. Some guys on that bus were nineteen or even twenty, having been held back several years in school. They were stupid and ruthless, and they picked on the younger kids mercilessly. I had my ears flicked to the color of a cherry by nasty bastard kids who could not pass the fourth grade years after going through puberty.

While I was academically capable of excelling, my grades were less than stellar. I loved learning and wanted to go to school, but I was feisty to a fault and was continually poked and prodded by the overgrown, mean-spirited, kept-back kids. I fought back with a vengeance. Outweighed and outreached, I'd lunge into my oppressors with a fire that provided me an edge. The more I fought, the better I got and the more I won, no matter how big my opponents were. But generally by the time the principal or a teacher arrived to break up the fight, I had been tagged as the aggressor. Eventually I was forced to drop out of the Dingess school system.

It wasn't all misery. We could wring laughter from simple events. One of my favorite memories involves my mom's brother, Uncle Merrick, who came home one day with a 1937 Chevrolet bakery delivery truck, a rust bucket with no side windows. Its massive headlights preceded it down the road. I adored that old thing. Eager to find out how all its parts worked, I tinkered with it and any other engine I could lay my hands on. And I got pretty good at maintaining and fixing motors. I was twelve when my father somehow acquired a red-and-white 1955 Ford Crown Victoria. Man, what a car! It wasn't hard learning to drive, because I loved just sitting in it, plus I had experience on a lot of farm machinery owned by our various neighbors.

Anything I didn't know about driving a Ford sedan I learned from my dad in the first half hour he owned it. From then on, I drove all over the county. I was four years underage for a driving license, but the closest police station was four hours away, and we never saw a cop in Dingess. Even if we had, one thing I've learned is that cops are often cheap to buy and don't want to work that hard. In some places, like Logan—only a half hour's drive from Dingess but several times bigger, and aspiring to be a real city—and Chicago Heights, they're even cheaper, but look at it from their perspective: their salaries are low, they're constantly in danger, and when they look at a guy with a new car and a sharp suit, it doesn't take much to turn them. Dingess in that sense wasn't different from the Heights except in size and the money that flowed through.[3]

Most of our drives would take us to my grandmother's house or to the local lumber mill. That Ford was a fun car, and I would love to have it today. But, like anything of value in the Hager family, we didn't have it long. A couple of months later Dad went on another binge and we lost the car to moonshine. I was almost as mad about losing the car as I was when he sold my puppy. Selling the car for booze was just one more in a very high pile of resentments I had built up against my dad and one more burden to the weariness I was amassing from living in an unbearably meager home in a miserable town.

Even in my petty, preteen mind, I knew that I was headed down the wrong path. If I didn't change my fighting, brawling ways or get away from Dingess entirely, I was headed for big trouble. My anger smoldered and was igniting a deep-seated resentment against poverty, violence, and stupidity. My vision of any decent future in Dingess was fast fading. I knew there had to be something better out there for me or I was doomed.

2. CHICAGO, UNCLE COLUMBUS, AND A NEW LIFE

I was thirteen in the summer of 1963 when my father's brother, Uncle Columbus, returned from Chicago to visit our home in Dingess. My father and his younger brother weren't close, and their temperaments were very different. Columbus, in contrast to my mean drunk of a father, was cordial, cautious, and subtle, thinking before he spoke. Like the rest of his brothers he was not highly educated, but he was obviously canny. He was about fifty, just under six feet tall and about 165 pounds, when I knew him. He married an Italian woman in Chicago, though I never got to know well her or any of his children. He always dressed well, and whenever he visited he spent a lot of time with me. Even then I could tell from his quiet self-assurance that he did not brook fools easily.

Columbus ran a tiny nightclub, a strip joint called the Hole in the Wall, on Dingess Street near our hometown in the 1940s and had made two attempts to get established in Chicago before moving there permanently in the 1950s. Once he did, he ran a club called the Blue Island Bar—about which we will hear more later. Coal mining, the only real money-making enterprise in West Virginia, has a history of wild swings in production and employment, and many from the state relocated to Chicago, Detroit, Cleveland, and other northern cities during the 1950s, when local jobs became scarce. Columbus didn't work in the mines, but the nightclub business suffered along with everything else, so he decided to go north too, landing in Chicago Heights. Now, he was back, with a nice suit, a good car, and money in his pocket.

The first time I recall hearing the name Sam Giancana was from Uncle Columbus. When I was ten years old and still small and obviously a child, he took me with him to a golf course, near Logan. It was early spring of 1960 when Columbus and I met a man on the golf course. I didn't pay much attention to him. I had never been on a golf course before, and there was more grass there than in all the yards in Logan put together. Columbus and the man chatted awhile, and the man gave him a bag. They said their good-byes, and the man left one way and we the other. I rarely asked Columbus a direct question, but I did that time.

"Who was that?"

"Sam Giancana," he replied. "Momo."

"Oh," I said, and let it go at that. I kept that strange name in the back of my mind. "Momo." I turned it over on my tongue. A memorable, almost musical name.

On the same day as the golf course visit, John F. Kennedy was campaigning in West Virginia and came to Logan. Columbus took me to the Hole in the Wall club there, on Stratton Street, where he had been a bartender at one time. Over and over the jukebox kept playing that damn song, Sinatra's "High Hopes," the theme of Kennedy's campaign. Not a lot of people in Logan had hopes, much less high ones, but the presence of the young, dynamic Kennedy gave the town a brief shot of energy.

The club was also a notorious whorehouse, and I later heard Kennedy had a woman there. There were police everywhere in Logan that day. The liquor stores had been cleaned out, as a vote could be bought in that county for just a little free booze. JFK ate at the Smokehouse restaurant nearby.

DURING A PREVIOUS visit to Dingess, Uncle Columbus had talked to my mother about my coming with him to Chicago for the summer. She wasn't so sure. He spent a good bit of time convincing her that spending a summer working for him would be a great opportunity for me to experience city life and have a summer job to boot. Columbus explained that if this summer worked out, I could come back to Chicago for the next few years. Finally, my mother agreed, and my father more or less acquiesced. Columbus told me to pack my things, and he would pick me up in the morning.

Packing for the summer took little time. I selected two pairs of underwear from the dingy three pairs I had; the third was too torn and dirty. I packed my only pair of bib overalls, which was standard dress for men and boys in Dingess, and two T-shirts and two pullover shirts—my entire wardrobe and two pairs of socks, each with a raggedy hole in the heel. I put one shirt, a pair of socks, and a wadded dollar bill my mother had given me on the bed for the next day and stuffed the rest into a brown paper shopping bag with two string handles on the top. I did not own a comb, a brush, or a toothbrush. My hair often looked odd, because when my mother would cut it the surges of pain through her hands from hoeing corn all day threw the scissors off.

I had trouble sleeping that night. Of course, I had trouble sleeping many nights, because so many of us were crowded into such a small house but also because I could often hear my mother moaning through waves of pain as leukemia began to tighten its grip. That night I barely slept for a different reason—my head was full of what I imagined Chicago would be like. Tall buildings, but also people with nice clothes, cars, a few extra dollars. I knew I would pass more people on the street in an hour than had ever lived in my whole town.

The next morning, right on time, Uncle Columbus pulled his 1961 Ford Sunliner into the driveway, waved to my mother on the porch, leaned over the passenger seat, and opened the door for me. I stopped to give my mother a warm but careful hug, promised to do everything she had told me, and bolted off the porch. I jumped in the car and put the brown bag on the floor between my feet. I was one happy kid. As my uncle backed the car down the dirt driveway I waved to my parents and brothers and sisters, and they waved back—enthusiastically at first and then more slowly in the rearview as my uncle shifted the car into drive and we started off to Chicago.

We pulled onto the on-ramp of West Virginia Route 10, and Uncle Columbus poked a finger into my bag of clothes. "Don't look like you packed much for the summer, kid. Whatcha got in the bag?"

"Not much. Two pair underwear, three shirts, pair of socks." I didn't need to tell him that that was all I owned. I glanced at his tailored suit and buffed shoes.

"Well, don't worry about it for one minute, kid. We'll get you a bunch of new stuff when we get to Chicago."

As the miles rolled by, my education began. "You're going to see a lot, and you're going to learn a lot, Charley, but whatever you see and do under my care stays between us. You got me?"

"Yes, sir." I made my voice as mature as I could manage.

"That's great, kid, because I'm going to make it my personal job to make sure you have one fine summer. OK?"

"Yes, sir."

We stopped occasionally to eat and use the bathroom as we made our way west, clipping along at a few miles over the speed limit. We stopped first at a truck stop, and for some reason I can still remember exactly what I had: a Coke and a cinnamon bun. That bun tasted so good that after the last bite I ran my finger around the empty plate and licked off the cinnamon-sugar.

"Want another?" Uncle Columbus said, smiling at me as he headed toward the cashier. "No, that's fine," I said, but I guess I wasn't very convincing. He looked at the cashier and pulled a ten-dollar bill from his wallet. "You'd better put another cinnamon bun in a bag for the trip. These kids get hungry."

"Yes, sir," she replied. "Four eighty-five." She took the ten and stuffed it into the register.

Climbing back in the shiny car, I said, "Thanks again, Uncle Columbus. That was good."

"Sure, kid, I'm glad you enjoyed it."

Sometimes we talked, but mostly I just listened as Uncle Columbus told me about his childhood, which was only a little better than my own. Looking back, I see that he was taking every chance he could to pass on good advice with each story, especially when he told me about things he did that he shouldn't have done. Grown-up things. He was incredibly honest, more so than a kid like me could expect. The few adults who had talked to me about their childhood made themselves sound too good. But Uncle Columbus seemed almost critical of himself.

It was a long drive, and I was tired and a little apprehensive but excited. I made a game of watching the moon swing into and out of the mirror on my side. One star shone a little brighter than the others; maybe it was my lucky star.

The lights of suburban Chicago began to flicker on in the western sky as the sun made its dying drop. My uncle weaved the car in and out of the gathering traffic until we finally turned onto South Blue Island Avenue. He pulled into a driveway in the alley beside what I would come to learn was his bar—the Blue Island—and parked just behind the building. "Here we are, Charley. Hope you like it."

I was nervous because I really wanted to make a good impression on Uncle Columbus's friends and the people he worked with. He took me by the hand and led me around the side of the building and in the front door. As we entered, voices from the bar and all around the dining room shouted out to Uncle Columbus. "Hey, gumba! How was the trip?" Another called out, "Hey, Silky!" I soon learned that that was Uncle Columbus's nickname. "Where'd you get the kid?" "Welcome back, boss," shouted another.

A fat Italian cook charged out of the kitchen, wiping her hands on a stained white apron. "Welcome, little Charley. How was the trip?"

Everyone called her Momma, and she pulled me hard into her huge belly and gave me a big, burly, grandmotherly hug. "Hey, he's a good-lookin' kid, boss." Uncle Columbus said hello all around, and it was clear he was well liked and respected, by both the people who worked for him and the dozen regulars who'd come in for a few drinks after work. The bartender, Tony, came around the bar and brought Uncle Columbus a shot and a beer and me a Coke. "Glad you're here kid; anything you want you just ask me. But not booze. The boss said no booze for you." He tousled my home-cut hair.

I looked around. Everyone I saw was bigger than life in my young eyes, and everyone was quick with a smile and a warm, pumping handshake or a big pat on the back or head-hooking hello. I had been in Uncle Columbus's world only a few minutes and I already loved it. In Dingess, strangers were met with guarded apprehension, and everyone, even neighbors of three generations, were greeted with only a reserved "howdy" or "how-do."

After a few introductions and more waves at customers, Uncle Columbus stuck his head into the kitchen. "Momma, get the kid a roast beef on a roll and a glass of milk, will ya?" He turned to me. "Sit over at that table, kid. Momma's going to get you a bite to eat. I'll be back in a minute."

I sat down where I was told and spent the next few minutes considering my new home. The room was dimly lit, and the bar seated about thirty patrons and ran down one side of the room to the right of the front door. I was sitting in the dining room, surrounded by dark wooden booths with green-shaded lights on each table and two fancy chandeliers above that cast a low, warm, golden light through the room. About a dozen ceiling fans kept the stale air moving. The floor was covered with a nondescript rug with deep signs of wear.

It wasn't long before Momma brought me a sandwich that balanced about a pound of lean roast beef on the bottom half of a roll and a massive bowl of potato chips on the side. She laid down napkin-wrapped silverware and asked if I wanted catsup, mustard, or mayonnaise with my sandwich. "No thanks," I said. "This looks too good all by itself." After two bites I found it was even better than it looked, with a strange but delicious flavor I later discovered was garlic.

It was paradise to me—exotic, noisy, boisterous, Italian. I glanced around and soon focused on Uncle Columbus, who was talking with a stout older man. I couldn't hear their words, but I could tell my uncle spoke with an intensity I had never seen in him. The older man had a helpless, apologetic look. He backed up a little as Uncle Columbus stuck a rigid index finger into his chest to punctuate the obvious dressing-down. Columbus whirled away from him, and the guy grabbed his hat and beat it out of the bar.

Uncle Columbus walked toward my table, and his face dissolved instantly from an angry scowl to a huge grin. He saw my nearly demolished sandwich. "How about that roast beef, kid? It looks like you're gonna take to this paisano chow."

"I've never had anything so good."

"Good, good! That's great!" he replied, with an enthusiastic clap on my shoulder. "Take your time! Take your time, kid, but when you're finished we'll go home."

I turned back to my sandwich. A big, broad-shouldered, Irish guy came in wearing a dark suit and a fedora sitting square atop his broad head over a reddish, flushed face. His grand entrance drew a rowdy response from the patrons at the bar, and one yelled out, "Christ, everyone, get your hands up on the bar! The Irish law is here."

"Well, top of the evening, Detective O'Brien!" said the bartender. "Who you gonna arrest tonight?"

"Looking at this sorry assortment of Dago deadbeats, I'm gonna arrest the lot of you!" He looked fierce for only a second. He threw his hat on top of the cigarette machine and marched up to the bar. "But before I get to the arresting part, I'm going to get myself a drink or two. Bartender, two shots and two beers and tell these other Wops to buy their own." That got a big laugh from the bar.

I listened to the back-and-forth and watched the newcomer being pulled into the group of Italians at the bar. What a place, I thought. They call each other the worst names and just laugh and give back as good as they get.

I would become friendly with a number of cops. Chicago was that way, the most corrupt city in the country then, maybe still is, and the cops didn't just look the other way when the Outfit did its business; they actively helped cover up crimes and skimmed a little of the Outfit's take in just about any criminal enterprise that would turn a buck. It was one of those mutual arrangements that I knew only too well from growing up in Mingo County. People in "Bloody Mingo," as it became known, had little education, a low quality of life, and little hope that their children would fare any better than their parents had.[1]

❧ ❧ ❧

My Uncle eased over to my table as I was wolfing down the last bit of roast beef and washing it down with the last sip of milk.

"You ready, kid?"

"Yes, sir," I said, pushing up from the table.

"Get enough food?" he asked.

"Plenty, thanks again."

"You're welcome, Charley." He put a hand on my shoulder and guided me to the door. The bartender yelled. "Good to meet you Charley; come back soon!" Several guys at the bar half turned and waved goodbye.

We climbed back into his car, and my uncle eased it out of the alley. He turned east up the street and didn't pick up speed but started looking for a parking place. He finally found one a block and a half from the bar. It was a tight squeeze, but he managed to get the car wedged into the spot with about a foot to spare, front and rear. I grabbed my bag and followed him into a nice apartment building with a brown awning over the entrance. He hit the button on the elevator, which opened immediately, and we got in and rode to the third floor. I followed him two doors down the hall and waited while he fumbled for the key and moved it around in the lock until it finally slid home.

I took a quick look around and was immediately awestruck. The walls were cream-colored and freshly painted, and shiny dark wood framed a broad line of windows that opened to the lights of the apartment buildings across the street. I saw people walking the street below, more people in one glance than ever lived in my little hometown.

"Wow!" was all I could manage.

"Thanks, kid," my uncle replied, looking pleased with my enthusiasm. "Come on, I'll show you your room." He walked in front of me, past a small dining room and into a narrow hall with a door on both the left and the right. He pushed open the one on the right and said, "This is it. This is your new home for the summer."

"Jeeze," I said, looking around at the neat and clean room, something I'd never experienced back in Dingess.

"All yours, kid. Your bathroom's through that door over there."

A real toilet, not an outhouse, and all mine. I looked at the clean tile, thinking it must have taken someone months to put those little black and white pieces together.

"Well, I'm gonna hit the hay," he said. "You'd better do the same. We're going to go shopping tomorrow and get you some clothes. We can't have you running around in that stuff you've been wearing. The Health Department would arrest me." More softly he added, "You're in the big time now, Charley."

"It feels like the big time, Uncle Columbus," I said. "The big big time."

"Good night, Charley."

"Good night, and thanks again," I said to Uncle Columbus's back as he closed the door behind him. "Thanks a whole, whole lot," I said to myself, as I unbuttoned the strap on my bib overalls and hurried into the bathroom. I pulled my shorts down and plunked my skinny butt down on the cool seat of my own damn toilet. This is going to be a good summer, I thought. Real good.

3. THE PRIDE OF DINGESS

I wasn't the only kid who dreamed of leaving our dingy little town. Dick Spry was seven years older than me, the oldest of four brothers, including red-haired twins. Dick looked just like them. You couldn't throw a dead cat without hitting one of those red-headed Sprys in our town. As an adult Dick was a little taller than me, under six feet, with a pasty white face covered with tiny freckles. His red hair was pulled straight back but had a little wave in it.

Some of the Spry cousins were much older than me, eighteen or nineteen years old when I was in fifth grade. I had five of the kids in my class, and Dick was one grade ahead of me in school. He and his brothers were men among boys and had to be promoted out of their grades based on age rather than school performance. Middle schools couldn't have two-hundred-pound men in the same class with ten-year-olds. The Spry boys were big, rough, and a pain in the butt. The teachers couldn't handle them. If they tried to discipline any of the Spry kids who had screwed up, Momma Spry would come down to the schoolhouse with a shotgun and a pistol and tell the school to get off the kids' back. Originally, the school we went to was named the Hager School because the Hagers owned it all until they lost it in the Depression. When the Sprys moved in they barely enhanced either the local economy or the gene pool.

The Spry family was all coal miners, and the kids were pretty much all ignorant except Dick. Dick was little and fast-tempered but by no means stupid. His daddy died young of a heart attack because he drank a lot. The older Spry kids came to school to play, not to learn. Dick and I would often play on the same baseball teams. He'd play first base and pitch, and I'd mostly play shortstop. He was a pretty good ball player and was usually the third or fourth selected in schoolyard games. In grammar school and high school Dick was a pretty good guy and didn't hassle a lot of other kids; he was light-years more refined than his brothers, who'd screw with you on the bus every day just for entertainment.

Just as I did, Dick had quite a bit of trouble with the teachers as he progressed through school; he never worked at it. He bumbled his way through middle school before dropping out, though he would come back briefly to high school before quitting completely. After he quit school for good he started to turn really bad. He thought he was invincible. He thought he could kick anyone's ass, and he'd never back down from a fight. According to rumor, Spry bought or stole explosives, mostly dynamite, from the mines in West Virginia and sold it to guys in the Ohio gangs. After he got out of school Spry picked up a big reputation as a bar and street fighter; he'd whack someone in the head with a pool cue in a heartbeat. It seemed like every kid in the school had a story about how Dick had whacked them with a pool cue.

The Spry family in general was a pretty screwed-up bunch. Almost all of Dick's family had been or would be killed in one way or another. His sister was run over by a car in Chicago, and the driver was never caught. One of the twins, Billy, died in a truck accident a thousand feet from his home, while he was street racing. His brother Cootsie was killed in a bar fight by the first guy who hijacked a plane to Cuba from West Virginia, the day after the hijacker had been released from prison. This all happened in a two-year period. Years in the future from our school days, but it seemed as though dark clouds followed everyone in that family.

I didn't know that one of their dark clouds would rain so heavily on me.

When he was about twenty Dick had his own little local club on the outskirts of Dingess. His bar was a small-town dump but kind of a fun place to drink, hang out, and get a feel for the local hick atmosphere. In the back of the joint and adjacent to Dick's room was one to play higher-stakes cards. Dick was ambitious. In those heady days of the late 1950s and early '60s, when so many West Virginians scattered to look for jobs, our dreams could as well have been about Pittsburgh, Detroit, Cleveland. All were big time to us. What I didn't know then was that Spry had a connection to Chicago, just as I did. I never spent time with Spry in Chicago, only on trips back to Dingess, but he would come to play a bigger role in my life, and I in his death, than either of us could have foreseen.

4. CLOTHES MAKE THE BOY

I woke the next morning in Chicago Heights with the sun streaming across the foot of my bed. I went to the window, craning my head to look up and down a street filled with early-morning delivery trucks. I could hear Uncle Columbus rattling around in the kitchen. I dressed and washed my face in my new sink and hurried to the door.

"Good morning, Uncle."

"Good morning, Charley. How'd you sleep?"

"Like a log, like an old dead log!"

"Get your shoes on; we're going out for breakfast and then we're going shopping."

We walked a block to a diner on the corner, and Uncle Columbus exchanged handshakes and hellos with the guy behind the counter and two or three people seated in a nearby booth.

"Where'd you get the kid?" the counterman asked.

Uncle Columbus put a strong hand on my shoulder. "This is my nephew, Charley Hager, and he's spending the summer with me. Oh, and by the way, anytime Charley comes in, give him what he wants, run the tab, and I'll pick it up next time I'm in. I'd consider it a favor."

After breakfast, my uncle set a brisk pace as we walked, covering two blocks quickly. He turned into a parking lot, toward a row of storefronts, and stopped at a clothing store that had mostly women's clothes in the window. A bell jingled as we pushed open the door, and a woman's throaty voice came from the back. "Look around; be right there." Uncle Columbus pointed me to the boys' section, and I started looking through the piles of shirts and pants. In a moment a middle-aged woman came from the back and gave Uncle Columbus a warm welcome. Columbus called to me. "Hey, Charley, come on over here. I got someone I want you to meet. Charley, this is Miss Paula Patsy, and she's gonna help you choose some new clothes so you can burn that other stuff, except the overalls, of course." I said an awkward, "How do, ma'am." She smiled. "Hi, Charley, let's look at some clothes."

We spent a little over an hour. Uncle Columbus continually chimed in, "Get it, kid" or "We'll take it, Paula." The pile of clothes on the counter grew truly impressive—eight shirts, five pairs of pants, eight pairs of socks, two pairs of shoes, a pair of sneakers, and eight pairs of Jockey shorts. I also got two toothbrushes, a hairbrush, deodorant, and some black Kiwi shoe polish in a black-and-gold flip-open can. Uncle Columbus paid Paula with a check, and after a brief thanks we loaded up the bags and headed home.

In the days that followed, the Chicago summer became blazing hot. I went to work sweeping up the Blue Island Bar and quickly became part of the busy flow of work there. Uncle Columbus kept a steady eye on me but also gave me a growing list of chores to do around the bar. I was happy to have the responsibility. My typical jobs in addition to sweeping were cleaning the tables and chairs and carrying racks of beer glasses back to the kitchen. My nickname became Chuckie or Kid, and I was the fast-footed gofer for everything the guys needed, which I really enjoyed because it meant I sometimes got to drive. Of course, I had no license. Back in those days all of us teenagers drove with no license when we could. Many of us country kids started working at mills or timbering operations as young as eight or nine, including driving trucks or heavy equipment; where we lived there was no one to enforce laws against it. (In fact, there was little law enforcement of any kind. My father's brother George, the eldest, literally got away with murder. But that's another story.) My uncle or one of the staff would have someone pick me up and give me a key to a certain car and tell me where to take it. And they would follow up to see that I did so.

Not once did my uncle tell me that something illegal was happening. "Look, kid, you see a lot of stuff going on around here, and I want you should keep your mouth closed about what you see and what you know, even to your family." In hindsight it was good sense on his part not to tell me more than I needed to know. He was usually serious and thoughtful, but when he did talk to me I paid attention because he talked about real-life things and I put much of what he told me to use almost immediately. He taught me not to trust anyone too quickly; to be friendly but not pushy, and to keep the other guy talking. He paid me a good allowance and told me to hold on to my money. He provided plenty of Cokes and food, but he didn't like me taking anything without asking. He would introduce me to someone, and after the guy was gone he'd tell me whether the guy was family, a good guy, a punk, or an asshole. Columbus knew that the people around the bar business would steal from him if he let them, so he left nothing to chance. I'd often see him working on his books, and I assume there were two sets, although my uncle never said so.

One day when I had just finished taking a rack of dirty glasses from the bar to the kitchen, Tony called me over. He sat me down at the bar and said, "Hey, Charley. How are things?"

"Great," I said.

"Got everything you need?" asked Columbus.

"Um . . . maybe?" Dumb me. I soon learned that my uncle's questions always had a point, a subtext, some little thing he wanted me to notice.

"Well, we got something that needs to be done. By someone with fast feet."

"You know, I've got fast feet," I replied, trying to sound mature.

"Well, we got something that needs taken care of, and we'd like you to take care of it."

"I'm your man," I said with a smile, my voice cracking only a little with a mixture of adolescent pride and guile.

"OK, good," said Tony. "At six o'clock, a guy will come here for you, and I'll introduce you to him. You go with him and he's gonna teach you about what we need done. The guy's name is Lorenze. He's gonna take you to dinner and then take you out for the job we got. OK?"

"Sure," I replied.

About an hour later a guy came into the Island and walked straight to the bar. He and Tony exchanged big Italian greetings, and Tony waved me over to the bar and said, "Charley, I want you to meet Lorenze. He's gonna take you to dinner. You do what he tells you. You got that?"

I put out my hand and said, "Hey, Lorenze, nice to meet you."

Lorenze looked at me. "Glad to meet you. Any kin of Columbus is a friend of mine. Let's go to dinner. The car's outside."

Lorenze and I went to dinner at a place in Chinatown. I had never eaten Chinese food before, so he ordered for me—strange small dishes with vegetables and rich brown sauce and pork. "I know Chinese food is a little different," he said, "but I think you're going to like it." And I did.

After we ate he took out a picture and a diagram and explained to me, in detail, how to hot-wire a car. We left the restaurant and walked out to the parking lot.

I've always been mechanically inclined and a quick study. Hot-wiring a car just means to bypass the ignition system and connect the battery directly to the starter by cutting the wires leading to and from the ignition switch and touching them together, sparking the starter. Chevrolets were easy to steal because their ignition system was so simple. General Motors cars were even easier—with them, the driver could pull the key out of the ignition while it was still turned to the starting position. If we sidled by and saw the ignition switch still turned it was simple to get into the car through the vent windows most cars had then. Or on most any car we could use a dent-puller tool to completely remove the ignition box under the steering wheel, then start the car with just a screwdriver. In any event, we always looked for ways to start the car without having to open the hood, which might attract attention.

Lorenze opened up his own car's hood, handed me a couple of tools and a few pieces of wire, and I practiced on his car about three times. "You got it down, kid; let's do it for real," he said.

I stopped for only a second to collect myself. Until now I suspected but could still deny to myself that I was doing anything illegal. This time it was, unmistakably. I wish I could say my conscience bothered me more than it did; but I was too far into my new life in Chicago to turn back. And I couldn't disappoint Uncle Columbus. And I couldn't go back to my miserable existence in Dingess.

We got back in Lorenze's car, and he drove about six blocks before pulling up near a dark corner. "After you take care of the job, I'll meet you here, but if you get stopped, you run the other way. Got it?"

"Got it," I replied. Lorenze drove around the next block and pulled up behind a '62 Cadillac sedan. "There you go, kid."

I wired the Caddy and left it there for another guy to pick up and walked back to the designated corner where Lorenze was waiting for me. "How did it go, kid?"

"Fine," I said, and we drove off. I knew I was doing something illegal and if I got caught I'd be in trouble. But it also felt good! I felt I'd done something brave and daring and that Uncle Columbus would be proud of me.

Lorenze must have reported my willingness and dexterity to Uncle Columbus. For the next job I was to pick up a car that was already hot-wired and drive it to another block where it would be picked up by someone else. I realized that having the job broken down this way prevented one guy from knowing how any particular car was stolen, so the job couldn't be followed easily by the cops. The cars would soon have a new, counterfeit serial number and be resold, without a trace.[1] Occasionally a guy wanted us to steal his car if, for example, he owed more on it than it was worth and wanted it to disappear. My education gradually began to account not only for hardware but for this kind of human nature. I was learning the ropes, a little at a time.

❧ ❧ ❧

THE BASEMENT OF the Blue Island was split into a large card room and some small rooms where local hookers took their clients for anything from a quickie to an all-nighter. The cathouse half of the basement could be entered only from the kitchen or the men's restroom. Once in a while there would be a scuffle and some shouting over a last-minute disagreement on price or services, and either Uncle Columbus or the bartender would hurry to settle it. About once a week a poker game was convened, with the usual players and one or two vouched-for outsiders, and it went on well into the night. The games were clearly illegal, but various guys were stationed around the bar to warn of approaching police, since not every cop was friendly. A series of rigged doorbells back to the poker room warned players of trouble. The doors of the brothel and the poker room could be locked from either side. But generally the guys had little to fear from the cop on the beat; Chicago police have always been deeply and notoriously willing to look the other way when it comes to organized crime.

I busted my ass, especially when there was a poker game. I was Mr. Downstairs, and I worked the lower end of the dumbwaiter, a two-foot by two-foot box on a series of pulleys that carried food and drinks from the bar and kitchen on the ground floor down to the card players in the basement, and returned their empty glasses and plates back up to the kitchen.

In addition to being bartender, a guy named Harry was also a guardian of the bar's illicit activities. His main job was to manage the brothel traffic in the basement, and only he had the keys. Harry always sat on the stool at the end of the bar and knew every one of the regulars; he kept the cathouse traffic flowing. Harry also took care of all transactions involving numbers running, sports betting, horse racing, hot-car action, and hot merchandise. He also doubled as the bouncer.

The various people around the bar had their assignments, and the people who worked for Uncle Columbus knew their roles and knew they'd better not screw up. Harry was watched by Uncle Columbus, who seemed to have eyes in the back of his head; he must have spent ten or twelve hours each day in his bar and restaurant. Harry and Uncle Columbus made sure nobody—and I mean nobody—went into the kitchen other than themselves and the people who worked there. Everyone was extra cautious to keep the bar and kitchen clean, because the liquor license was dependent on it. Without a liquor license, the Blue Island was nothing.

The bar hosted several pay phones through which bets and numbers were called in from and to the various bookies who were always hanging around the bar, taking bets on numbers, sports games, horse races, and anything else anyone was willing to bet on. Throughout the day, dozens of delivery guys would come and go, bringing in or taking out envelopes and various-sized brown paper packages packed with money or tickets.

The Blue Island was more than just a neighborhood bar and restaurant and a center for gambling, prostitution, and money laundering. It was also an informal meeting place for guys in the Outfit. I didn't know anything about organized crime at that age, but the Outfit, or the Syndicate, or the Chicago Mob—it went by several fearsome names—was and is legendary, with roots in the days of Al Capone. And in West Virginia, as I came to learn. It was near the height of its power in those days, with tentacles reaching all over the Midwest and beyond, and into every type of criminal endeavor imaginable. The Outfit claimed control of crime from south of Chicago east to Indiana and west to Iowa, with branches into Appalachia.

Maybe because of the movies, people envision upper-level guys running around in black cars and hanging out in nightclubs. But that's not the way the Outfit worked. Sure, some of the street-level guys were punk hoods, but the upper-level guys acted like businessmen, family men. The Mob respected order and discipline, and demanded it from those who had even midlevel responsibilities.

In the years I worked for the Outfit, before I landed in jail, I recognized the critical rules of operation. First, the Outfit was almost but not entirely Italian,[2] and most of the guys I knew were dedicated to their families and went home to them every night. Second, because they were family guys they didn't like drugs, which hurt kids; so if you were a member of the Outfit, at least in the years I came to know it and among the people I worked with, you didn't use drugs and you didn't sell drugs. And if you did you were subject to getting talked to, or whacked. At first I thought it was because people make bad decisions when they use drugs, but I came to see that the reason was more cynical: drug-crime charges were harder to get dismissed in court, and drug profits were controlled by a different gang. And the penalties for dealing were greater than those for most of our theft operations.[3] You could drink, but you never wanted to get the reputation of being a drunk. The Outfit was ruthless and unforgiving, ruling by fear and murder and maintaining and extending its territory and power by the same means. You might be warned of a minor infraction of their rules, but you might also get offed without even a warning.[4]

THE PUBLIC FACE of the Blue Island was legit, and it was only one of the Outfit's many gathering centers, but a quiet, curious kid with a well-connected uncle could learn a lot just by standing around. I guess Columbus figured the Outfit offered me a better future than Dingess. I would grow to be a close confidante with his guys, never made as such, but someone who could be trained the way the Outfit wanted its workers trained. Chicago-based researcher John Binder compares the Mob to a Fortune 500 company: "It's important in management to groom people," he said. "The Outfit is good at it; they've shown the ability to bring people up."[5] And bring me up the Outfit did, in the sense of becoming my substitute family. For now, with my father disabled and alcoholic, and my mother's health failing rapidly back home, all I had in front of me was Uncle Columbus. "Hey kid, watch yourself," he said. "It's a jungle out there." Columbus must have felt it was his job to lead me through that jungle. He was introducing me to a life of crime, but nothing could be worse than the alternative—a dirt-poor and miserable existence with no hope and no future. So, just a few short months out of the sump of misery that was Dingess, I got to see more of the world than I imagined existed—the "real" world of skyscrapers and Lake Shore Drive and pretty girls but also the ruthless otherworld of organized crime. I was to find that Uncle Columbus was a small but important employee of a profitable multinational conglomerate where money flowed freely and good food and clean flush toilets were commonplace. In Uncle Columbus's world, everyone walked around with money in their pockets and plunked it down easily enough to buy not only their needs but their wants. In Dingess people looked nervous when they produced a wadded bill or two from a pocket of their bib overalls, and there was no such thing as extra food; unlike Chicago, there was no "more where that came from." In Dingess that's all there was.

❧ ❧ ❧

ALL TOO SOON my summer in Chicago came to a close. During that time, prodded by Uncle Columbus, I had sent my mother two postcards and she had sent me two letters. She was upbeat. Overly so, I came to learn. When the summer was over, Uncle Columbus bought me more new clothes and shoes and made sure I had cash in my pocket—a hundred dollars, a fortune in those days. I hid it as well as I could lest it turn into paternal alcohol. I was certain things would be different when I got back to Dingess. I would be an equal now with the other kids, with new clothes and dollars in my pocket.

On the third Sunday in August Uncle Columbus sent me home with an associate named Lorenzo (not Lorenze—so many new names and people!) who was heading to Washington, DC, and detoured to drop me off in Dingess.

For the next few years I would split my time between Chicago and home. I traveled to Chicago a few weeks at a time, and my marginally illegal activities there became more and more routine, as I grew bigger, stronger, and more canny about carrying out Columbus's orders.

But I wasn't at home in either world, and every trip to Dingess took me back through that damned tunnel. There was opportunity in Logan— don't get me wrong—for a young would-be hood; but the real money lay north-northwest, by those big lakes. And my work there took advantage of my natural skills.

You don't think about danger when you're young, but people get hurt doing the kinds of things I was doing. Or killed. It wasn't my own mortality that I would meet in the Heights, but it may as well have been.

5. HOME AGAIN

My vision of returning to Dingess with new confidence was shaken immediately, as I found my mother increasingly frail from leukemia. The people of Dingess lined up for hours to donate their blood, but she slowly got sicker through the long fall and winter of 1967 as my disabled father spiraled farther down into a mean alcoholic void. My mother's need for nineteen blood transfusions sorely taxed the small hospital's resources. But when the call went out for blood donors, the entire county, it seemed, lined up in the rainy West Virginia winter to share theirs with one of their most respected women. The tiny and impoverished population of Dingess knew their neighbors and respected good people, regardless of what they had or didn't have. Coal miners and their families did what they could; my mother was showered with love from those who knew the sacrifices she had made for an enormous brood.

In 1966 and '67, after summers with Columbus in the Heights, my mother's illness forced me back to my old life temporarily—school and working summers in a sawmill in Man, West Virginia, about twenty miles from my home in Dingess. I bumbled through the school year until December 1967, doing just enough work to get by. Not long before Christmas my mother, my rock and protector, was given six months to live. The imminent loss became more real and nearly unbearable as I watched her die little by little. She faded to a gaunt, gray ghost against clean white hospital sheets. Despite her increasing illness Mom tried to keep her anguish from me. But before a smile could blossom fully on her lips a surge of pain would pull them into a grimace. As she endured each of her final days she did everything she could to let me know that she loved me and would watch over me after she was gone.

She died at forty and had two dollars and thirty-four cents in her pocketbook. Even today, I wonder how a supposedly all-knowing and benevolent God could bestow such a harsh life on one so kind. As I watched her approach the last hours of her life, I started thinking of the days ahead and what losing her would mean to the rest of the family. She provided love and support for ten children while keeping a drunken, mean man at bay. There was no replacement for her in the lives of her kids. My sister Della, still a teenager, stepped up to be the caregiver for the family, but we knew there would be little or no help from our father. He would finish life as he had lived it, with a pint of moonshine at his lips, stealing from everyone in the family to dull the physical and emotional pain of his miserable life. Looking back at those dark and empty days following my mother's death, I often wondered if I should have stayed in Dingess to help Della with my brothers and sisters instead of fleeing to the shelter of Uncle Columbus in Chicago. But I didn't.

In 1965, when my mother was diagnosed with leukemia, we had moved to Logan to be near the hospital. It was barely a step up. I began attending Logan Central Junior High. By age fifteen I had developed the habit of listening more than I talked, and many conversations in Logan centered on local politics. The first rumor I heard as a new young resident of Logan was that the sheriff, Don Chafin, bribed his mother to switch political parties; it seemed that every politician and his mother could be bought. And the more government project money came down, the more the politicians owned the voters. I would come to regard the political systems of both Chicago and southern West Virginia as equally corrupt, and in both the people feared and respected a netherworld of crooks, criminal insiders, political charlatans, and bosses.

At fifteen I couldn't pay much attention to Logan politics. I had my hands full just surviving, growing into a man who had to defend his own. I hung around too many bars and billiard parlors with too many guys of questionable reputation. One day I had an unfortunate confrontation with a gentleman—a term I use loosely—named Joe in a pool hall. I won the game, but Joe reached down and snatched my five-dollar winnings from the table. There was little I could do because he was six-feet-seven and outweighed me by nearly 150 pounds. Joe told his buddy to rack the balls. I wanted my money. When Joe stretched out over the pool table to break the rack of balls, opportunity knocked. As he went for the opening shot I turned my pool cue around and grasped it around the narrow end. I took a long sweeping backswing, smashed the thick end of the cue into the bridge of Joe's nose and then broke what was left of the cue across his head. He fell like a stone on the pool table, and I snatched my five dollars from his pocket. His buddy ran to get help, and they took Joe to the hospital.

A few days later Joe and I went before the infamous Logan judge "Onion Head" Chambers, named for his massive bald dome. Onion Head said, "Will the defendant please stand?" I stood, barely of average height. Onion Head said, "Will the plaintiff please stand?" and Joe stood, all six-feet-seven and 275 pounds of him. Looking at us in disbelief, Onion Head asked if I had gotten my five dollars back, and I said that I had.

Old Onion Head looked at Joe. "You know you robbed this guy. Do I need to say more?" I actually felt a bit guilty because Joe really looked rough, and I figured that, with a full swing and throwing even my scrawny weight into the cue, I had to have caused some real damage. This was poolroom justice at its best. While I was not charged, I was told that it would be wise for me to leave Logan, so my Aunt Emma took me to Mingo County, where I entered Lenore High School. The new schedule was miserable. I had to be up at five in the morning and didn't get home until five in the evening. The bus rides were daily endurance tests. I found school dull, and escape to Chicago looked better and better as the school year crept by.

The Man Lumber Company was my first trial at hard labor—my trial by sweat, by discipline, by creating a man's body from a sixteen-year-old boy's and learning how to make what Loretta Lynn called "a poor man's dollar." And that's exactly what I made—a dollar a day. I was not happy working that sawmill; it was a god-awful job. But I have to admit it was a character-building job, like joining the Army, with long hours and days away from home.

Just as in my school days, the smaller and younger kids at the mill were continually harassed and bullied by the older and bigger kids. This behavior seemed to be some kind of dirt-farm rite of passage for both the abused and the abusers. Being smaller, and probably feistier, than most kids at school, I was constantly picked on and harassed by the bigger kids, especially the nineteen- and twenty-year-olds who had been held back for several years: the Sprys, except for Dick. It was the same in the lumber mill. Fortunately, I had grown up boxing with a lot of kids around Dingess. Though I was still small, I got better and better at fighting the bigger kids, and I was quick to fight anyone who was teasing and harassing me. The more I fought, the better I got at it, and the better I got at it, the more I was left alone.

As a result every year I learned to fight bigger and bigger kids and started winning more and more fights. I didn't always win, but I won often enough and inflicted enough damage so that the other kids didn't want to fight me if they didn't have to. Much the same thing happened when I was working at the Man mill. There's something extremely educational about working with kids from a bunch of different towns, even towns that were fairly close to where you were raised. Living night and day among kids from different towns, you quickly learn what's acceptable and what's not. You learn the older kid's language. You learn that the f-word can be twisted into nouns, verbs, adjectives, adverbs, and almost any other part of speech, endless variations. You learned to put it in strange combinations.

The mill week was long. Mill operators sent a bus to get us on Sunday evening and to take us home Friday night. We worked ten-hour days for a dollar a day. But they fed us well, three meals a day, and we had barracks-type bunks to sleep on. For us poor West Virginia country kids it was exciting but scary, with a fast exchange of information from the older teenagers to the younger teenagers, telling them more or less reliably what to expect. The big kids passed down information during meals or bullshit sessions in the evening, sometimes one-on-one and others one-on-two or -three or -four. The younger ones got a flood of information about sex, some of it accurate and helpful, some of it bogus and outright confusing. Lots of the older kids smoked, and many of the younger ones took it up to feel like big shots. Me? I didn't much like it, and I was smart enough to know that I should not waste even a dollar of the six or seven bucks I brought home each week. Those few dollars often made the difference in whether my brother and sisters and I could eat.

Most of the other kids my age at the sawmill couldn't afford to buy cigarettes either, but I guess they didn't give a shit and bought them anyway.

DURING THE LAST month of the second summer I worked at the sawmill, an older worker named Cannonball Jeffries and I spent weekends posted at a small guard shack at the entrance to the mill. One night, Cannonball and I were sitting by the road outside the mill, shooting the shit and killing time at the end of a two-mile stretch of rural macadam where locals, especially bootleggers, liked to test their cars for speed. From what we saw on several evenings, they reached crazy speeds in that stretch. This particular evening we watched as a fire-engine-red convertible approached our perch at raceway speeds. As the car got nearer we could pick out two teenage girls with their long hair flying in the wind. They had to be going eighty, and the light convertible was weaving as they came flying toward us. By pure happenstance, a Chinese doctor at Man Hospital, who had one of those James Dean Porsches, was catching up with the dangerous duo, traveling much faster than the girls.

Next to the road and a few hundred feet from where we sat were a house and the stump of a beech tree cut down to build the house. As the Porsche caught up with and started to pass the red convertible, both cars vied for the right-of-way. Inevitably, the Chevy was forced off the road at full speed; it hit the stump and flipped into the house, coming to a rest upside down with all the doors sprung open. Both girls were thrown from the car, and it didn't take a medical degree to see that both were dying almost instantly. One girl's head and jaw were stuck in the side of the house.

We rushed to help, but too late. I held the older girl in my arms while she lost pint after pint of blood. Cannonball held the other as she died. The doctor turned his Porsche around and stopped and examined both girls. He checked for a pulse on the younger girl's leg, and said, "She's gone." He looked at the girl in my arms and said, "I'm afraid she's gone, too. Please stay with them while I get help. It's only two miles away." I said, "Sure," and Cannonball and I held the two bodies in our arms and waited about forty-five minutes for an ambulance to arrive. We turned over the two dead girls to the medics. The doctor took our names and addresses, and we walked back to the lumber mill. Later we found out that the girls were the twin daughters of J. Ned Grubb, an attorney and eventually a judge—though he would come to serve time in prison, just like me.[1] Ned Grubb would play a big role later in my life, when I was accused of murder.

6. AN UNMADE MAN

I knew little about the Outfit when Columbus brought me back with
him more or less permanently when I was sixteen. I knew little of crime
other than petty theft, though in Mingo County crime and corruption
were like water to a fish. I would learn about both Chicago and my home
area in the years to come, as I traveled back and forth, and decided they
really differed only in scale and ambition.

The Chicago Outfit I was introduced to wasn't like the Mafia you see in
movies, run by a few families. Chicago's crime hierarchy had higher-ups
who weren't exclusively Italian and who had evolved a more practical approach to management, beginning before the 1920s but nourished by the
success of Al Capone's racketeering enterprises during Prohibition. Capone
also pioneered new ways to bribe or intimidate local law enforcement, the
kind of lessons that would be applied, I came to learn, even down into my
"bloody" Mingo County.

When Capone was jailed on tax evasion charges, he turned the organization over (at least nominally) to Frank Nitti, though the real head was
reported to be Paul Ricca, who would run the Outfit for decades. He oversaw
its expansion into new enterprises (juice loans, gambling) and new territo-
ries in the Midwest but also in the burgeoning California and Hollywood
markets. Ricca's control of labor unions gave the Outfit a leg up on the
fast-growing movie industry.[1]

Ricca and his underboss, Tony Accardo, helped propel the Outfit into
counterfeiting, slot machines, and drug smuggling in the 1940s. A canny
businessman, Accardo saw to it that brothels gave way to "call girls," and
legitimate businesses covered many tracks. Accardo ensured that Las Vegas
casinos used slot machines approved by the Outfit, and the Outfit laundered
millions of casino dollars.[2] In the 1950s they began to recruit new talent,
such as the members of the extremely violent Chicago "Forty-Two" gang,
which included a young Sam Giancana.[3] He would go on to be arrested

37

more than seventy times for a staggering variety of offenses: contributing to the delinquency of a minor, assault with intent to kill, larceny, bombing, gambling, and much more.[4] Ricca and Accardo took a lower profile in the late 1950s, though they exerted indirect control. In the early 1960s the Outfit reportedly even got involved in the CIA's ill-fated plans to overthrow Cuba's Fidel Castro.[5] Giancana had lost a lot of money when his Cuban "business interests" fell to Castro. Under Giancana's lead, Chicago experienced "a wave of underworld violence unparalleled in Chicago since the days of Al Capone. . . . The corruption-ridden Chicago police department has been unable or unwilling to keep the crime syndicate in check." As one reporter put it, "In this state, Giancana gets whatever he wants. And nowadays his syndicate wants everything."[6] This included a get-out-of-jail-free card, apparently. "[O]n three occasions when federal authorities had Giancana in a tight spot, they let him out of it. They blocked his indictment on wiretap charges, declined to cross-examine him about his Mafia activities when they had the chance, and turned down the opportunity to send him back to jail."[7]

The feds were applying more and more heat to the organization, however, and an intense FBI intelligence effort in 1963 kept Giancana and everyone he met with under constant scrutiny; the effort revealed the existence of a Cosa Nostra "gangland council" that united organized crime across nine cities.[8] Accardo's man Giancana, brought in when legal troubles forced them to take a lower profile in the late 1950s, was now bringing too much attention to the Outfit. For one thing, in 1963 he had the gall to sue, unsuccessfully, the FBI and the Cook County sheriff for harassment ordered by Bobby Kennedy.[9] (He claimed the surveillance violated the "sacred institution of the home by using high-powered cameras."[10]) To bring the suit, he had to testify and would thus be subject to cross-examination, but the Justice Department ordered the U.S. attorney handling the case not to question him.[11] He seemed beyond the reach of mere-mortal law enforcement.

Giancana "drove a pink Cadillac . . . [and] wore sharkskin suits, alligator shoes, silk shirts, a gold monogrammed belt buckle," and, symbolizing a lifelong Italian friendship, "a star sapphire pinky ring that was a gift from Frank Sinatra." Sinatra introduced Giancana to Judith Campbell Exner and thus into the orbit of John F. Kennedy.[12] Giancana reportedly told Exner, "Listen, honey, if it wasn't for me, your boyfriend wouldn't even be in the White House."[13] Giancana thought, wrongly, that his "in" at the highest level of government would protect him, and he felt double-crossed when attorney general Bobby Kennedy began to crack down on organized crime.[14]

In addition to his flashy lifestyle, Giancana's high-visibility ruthlessness was well documented; he is reported to have once said, "Seven out of 10 times when we hit a guy, we're wrong. But the other three guys we hit, we make up for it."[15] During Giancana's reign from 1957 to 1966, there were seventy-nine Chicago mob murders, while only twenty-four occurred in the eight years that followed.[16]

In 1966 I was sixteen and just beginning to make a place for myself in Chicago, but things were changing way up in the organization and in the Chicago area. That was the year Giancana refused to testify before a grand jury, and he would spend a year in jail, losing control of Chicago's crime empire, before fleeing to Mexico.[17] He spent seven years in exile, mostly in a Mexico City penthouse but with side trips to South America and Iran. By late 1972 he was said to have "gone mod" and was described as "the Ambassador-At-Large for the crime syndicate." Always higher-profile than the Outfit would like, he became "an underworld dandy" favoring "flared trousers, sweater shirts, high-heeled boots," sporting a beard and moustache and sometimes a toupee.[18]

Giancana would make the fateful decision to return to Chicago in 1974, perhaps forced out of Mexico by authorities there, and the even more fateful decision to testify to the feds, about which more will come later.

In the 1960s the civil rights movement challenged the old political order in Chicago,[19] and law enforcement became less cozy with the Outfit when Cook County got a new sheriff in 1962 and "appointed incorruptible Chicago police officer Art Bilek as Chief of the Sheriff's Police."[20] But the Outfit was finding new revenue streams. It began highly profitable chop-shop operations, which created a need for reasonably sober, dependable drivers who were good with the mechanics of cars; young men such as myself. The 1960s saw the introduction of new personnel who did not come from the Heights, as was historically true, but were brought in as new blood by some trusted low-level Outfit associate such as Columbus. We newcomers had the advantage too of not being known by the local heat.

That's the world I was dropped into, one of violence. When I arrived in the Heights, still wet behind the ears, I was given the most simple and mundane tasks, just to show I could be counted on. One little job led to a little bigger one, which led to a little more responsibility, which led to the book you're reading now. At each step, with nowhere else to go and not much education, I didn't see any way forward but to push ahead and do the best I could. The Outfit still had plenty of low-level retail work that never touched its glamorous Vegas or Hollywood connections. Columbus was only a small cog in an immense machine, but to me he was a man of the world, big-time, with money in his pocket and respect. I wanted that too. I figured as long as I did what he said, I'd be fine. He said as long as I kept my head down and my ears open, I'd be fine. And for a time, he was right.

7. A LICENSE TO STEAL

My first summers with Uncle Columbus, I was too young for a driver's license, but I got one the day I turned sixteen. It was a formality. I'd always loved cars and been handy with them. A year later, I got my first car, a 1957 Corvette, which Uncle Columbus helped me buy. I thought I was a real hotshot. Now that I had my own car, Uncle Columbus had me doing more and more errands and moving more and more brown-bag packages around South Chicago.

Several times in my visits to Uncle Columbus in Chicago Heights I went with him or someone who worked with him into Chicago proper. I have to admit that I was in awe of all the glass storefronts and massive buildings. Growing up, my horizon stretched no farther than the foot of a "holler" and no higher than a couple of stories. I hadn't believed something like the Chicago skyline existed.

By the time I was working for Uncle Columbus in the summer of 1968, I was eighteen and Chicago was booming. I had just returned from an errand when I was given instructions that a brand-new brown-and-white Chevy sedan would be parked at a corner on North State Street in Chicago. As usual, I was given the key to the ignition but not the one to the trunk. I was told that one of the locals would drive me to the car and there would be a package in the front seat which I was to give to Uncle Columbus in his bar. Then I was to drive the car to the corner of Cicero Avenue and 179th Street in West Chicago, leave the car unlocked in front of a gray townhouse with the ignition key under the front seat, and take the bus home. I had it down by now. The guy who drove the car away from the gray townhouse didn't know I had left it there or where it originally came from. I didn't know where the car I picked up in front of the drugstore had come from, or who left it there or what was in the trunk. I didn't know where it was going. I didn't need or want to know. As a result, none of us could be called to testify about it, really. I didn't realize that job was something like an audition.

41

Near the end of my third summer with Uncle Columbus, when I got back from a run and returned to Uncle Columbus's bar about nine thirty at night, I found the place almost empty except for two unsteady barflies bending over their beers and talking enthusiastic nonsense. But this night was different. Uncle Columbus was sitting in a corner booth at the far side of the bar reading the paper. When he saw me, he yelled out, "Hey, kid, grab yourself a beer and come on over." He'd never offered me a beer before, but that didn't worry me, because I knew he had my best interests in mind and always would have. Lately, he had been talking about getting me out of the penny-ante operations associated with his bar and in with some important guys who could help me make some real money. When I sat down, Columbus and I rehashed the run I'd just come from, by way of small talk. Uncle Columbus looked straight at me, which he seldom did, and said, "Look, kid, I kinda like having you around 'cause you're a sharp kid, you do what you're told, and you keep your mouth shut. I trust you like you was my own kid." I can't tell you how good that made me feel, because I had great respect for Uncle Columbus, respect and real affection for my mentor, something that was missing with my own father.

"I think I got somethin' you might be interested in. A couple of days ago, I got wind of the fact that a couple of big shots in Chicago Heights were looking for a chauffeur, a guy who could do what he was told to do and keep his mouth shut. I let them know that I had a nephew who was a cool kid and could be trusted to keep his mouth shut. So, Thursday, I want you to go up to the Heights, show up at Vergie's Lounge about eight o'clock, have a drink at the bar, and when nobody's within ear shot, you tell the bartender that you're the kid your Uncle Columbus sent to try out for the chauffeur job." Vergie's Lounge was on Chicago Road (Illinois Route 1), in south Chicago Heights, just up the street about a quarter mile from the old Vagabond Lounge, the brown building that served as a bar and a brothel.[1]

Now, I'd been around long enough to know that a chauffeur for the Outfit is more than a driver. This may be my big break, I thought. I was still going back and forth between the Heights and Dingess, but the latter was looking less and less like home now that I'd had a taste of the big city. I needed work, however. I told my uncle, "Thanks, sure, I'll give it a shot; sounds like that might lead to something pretty good."

I had begun diligently learning my way around the complicated and immense (compared to Dingess) street grid of Greater Chicago. I developed the habit of keeping track of turns—this building on my left, that one on my right—and developed a sense of direction that came in handy for chauffeuring. The guys I had seen driving for the Outfit were the original Uber—they'd take you anywhere in that wonderland of Chicago you wanted, no questions. I was also quick to learn the best ways to get around and to avoid the areas that belonged to another gang. I knew I could handle this job.

"No problem, kid," Uncle Columbus said, and he looked at me in what I thought was a fatherly way. "I hope it works out for you." That was the night Columbus seemed to be handing me off to the larger work of the Outfit.

As instructed, I drove from the Blue Island about thirty minutes to Chicago Heights, which was known as a major headquarters of organized crime in South Chicago. I arrived at Vergie's Lounge a little before 8 P.M. and eased onto a stool at the end of the bar. The place was pretty crowded, and the jukebox was playing the Temptations' "My Girl."

I ordered a beer and tried to act as cool as I could, especially with the bartender. Around eight thirty the stools on either side of me were vacant and the bartender was leaning against the back of the bar, wiping a glass with a white towel. I waved him over and said, "Hey, my name is Charley Hager, and my Uncle Columbus said I was to tell you that he wanted me to try out for the chauffeur's job."

"Well, OK," the bartender said, "we were expecting you, Charley. Just hang loose, there'll be a guy, comin' in about ten, who'll give you some instructions. For now, welcome to Vergie's Lounge, Charley, have a drink on us." The guy appeared a little before ten and said his name was Tony. He questioned me for almost an hour, plying me with a couple of beers, and then said, "OK, Hager, come to the B&B Garage at the corner of Chicago Road and Hickory Street tomorrow morning; we're going to show you a route we want you to drive for the Mexican Independence Day Parade."

The next morning I parked in front of the B&B Garage and walked into the front office. Tony was waiting in a rickety customer chair that had seen better days and said, "Good timing, kid; come on, let's get my car, you'll have a better one tomorrow." Tony said, "Four important officials are going to get in your car here and you go down Chicago Road for about eleven blocks as fast as the high-school band in front of you is going." He showed me where one of the officials was going to get out and said I should take the rest of the guys back to the Vergie's.

When I showed up at the B&B well before the start of the parade, I almost pissed my pants when I found out that my first job as a chauffeur for the Outfit was to drive Nick Pagoria, the mayor of Chicago Heights, up

Chicago Road in the Mexican Independence Day Parade. They gave me a red 1960 Cadillac convertible belonging to a guy named Cadillac Joe to drive, and I polished it to a shine before the mayor got in.

The parade started at the corner of Chicago Road and Hickory Street, and ended at the other end of Chicago Road at the Liberty Restaurant. I looked back at not only the mayor but also a Who's Who of organized crime in the Heights: Albino "Dago Tony" Berrettoni, who, I later found out, ran the gambling operations for the Outfit; Al Pilotto, the undisputed boss of the Chicago Heights mob; and in the back Nick D'Andrea, with Tootsie Palermo riding shotgun. Everyone was smiling like crazy and waving to the crowd. I kept my hands on the wheel and did my best to keep to the engine-stall pace of the parade. After a quarter mile or so I got the hang of it.

The Heights crew of the Outfit controlled all organized crime south of Chicago, all the way to Kankakee and Joliet. The crew was run by Pilotto. Al Tocco was a strong number two, and Nick D'Andrea was number three. I learned only gradually how deep-rooted Nick's family was in the area.[2] Joe Barrett Jr., the guy who ran the Vagabond Lounge, was obviously one of the upper-level sidemen. These four mainly controlled the gang I worked for. Pilotto, however, reported to Joey "Doves" Aiuppa and River Forest's own Tony "Big Tuna" Accardo of the Chicago Syndicate, and they, in turn, had national connections.[3] I didn't work directly with Accardo; he was an old-time Outfit guy, working his way up over four decades.

At the end of the parade, the mayor got out and was shaking hands with a bunch of well-wishers, and Tootsie Palermo said, "OK, kid, take us to Vergie's. You know where it is?"

"Yes, sir, I do," I shot back.

"Yes, sir," Tootsie smiled and said, mocking me. "Hey, the kid thinks I'm a big shot. Look out, Al, I may be after your job!"

"You can have it, Tootsie."

We got to the lounge in about five minutes, and everyone piled out.

It was a great day, and I think I handled it OK because everyone thanked me and said I did a good job. As he got out of the car, Al Pilotto grabbed my shoulder and said, "I'm gonna have a few jobs for you sometime next week, Charley, OK?"

"Yeah, I'm great."

"Find a place to park out front; come on in the lounge and have a beer."

After a beer at Vergie's we moved on to the Vagabond. The Vagabond Lounge was a well-known bar and brothel, housed in a beautiful and ornate former car dealership, the Flatiron Building, which also served as a taxicab station[4]: a full-service establishment, in other words. Barrett was one of the main guys running it. He was a second-generation (at least) member of the Outfit. The Vagabond was the chief hangout for Nick and his crew as well as some of the higher-ups. When I went into the lounge I didn't join Tootsie and Nick at a table but went straight to the bar, ordered a beer, and thought back on the day. I decided then the Heights would be my permanent home. Why? Well, first, the area around Uncle Columbus's bar was getting to be infiltrated by more and more Mexicans who were taking over the neighborhoods from the Italians, and soon the competition would become even more fierce and bloody; I could not see a big-deal future for me there. I also thought the life around the Outfit was more exciting. Finally, I thought there was a lot of money to be made in the Heights. I decided to get my own apartment, with Columbus's blessing.

A week later I went to Uncle Columbus's bar, collected my odds and ends, and drove back to the Heights. I was eighteen, and Chicago was swirling with the famously rough Democratic National Convention, antiwar protests, and much more. The previous year's "Summer of Love" was still in full swing in the Heights. Drugs were plentiful, though I wasn't attracted to them, and beautiful young women were doffing their bras as the music shifted from Sinatra to Hendrix. Busy making my own way, I was oblivious to all that. At eighteen, I was a full-grown man, with a job, a car, a place to live, and a mentor in Uncle Columbus. I had lost my father to alcohol long ago, then my mother to leukemia. And now, as Columbus's direct role in my life waned, I seemed ready to be on my own.

But I wasn't really on my own. Because I'd started so young, Nick and his brother Mario took me under their wing and began teaching me some of the finer points of their work. They also always seemed to be looking over my shoulder and nudging me in the right direction.

I rented a small place at 1608 Aberdeen in Chicago Heights, two blocks from Nick's home, and got a legitimate job at Desoto Chemicals, a Sears and Roebuck subsidiary. The change felt good. I was going somewhere; I was going to be somebody. But I had no idea about the price I would pay for my rising role in the Outfit. I had a lot to learn about the Mob, and some of what I learned would later scare me senseless; the Outfit is a way of life, not a part-time job. I also found that my dreams about a fast rise to power in the Outfit were unrealistic. These guys trusted no one until he'd served a long apprenticeship and handled a lot of small-time jobs. And even then, I would learn over and again as guys came and went, the leaders of the Outfit were your friends only as long as you were useful to the organization.

The beautiful and famous (or infamous) Flatiron building, originally a car dealership but eventually the second Vagabond Lounge. *Courtesy Constantine D. Vasilios and Associates, Ltd.*

Blazen Sun, one of my most successful horses, in a photo finish. I'm at the far right. I had just come from my Amoco station, as you can see by my uniform. *Charles Hager collection.*

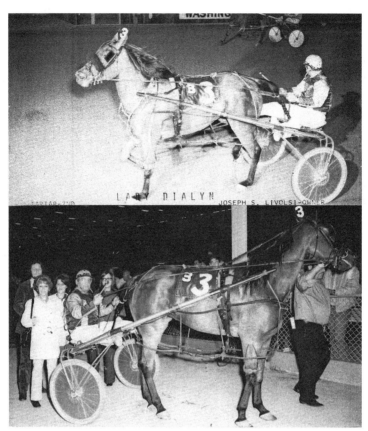

Lady Dialyn, a great horse on a winning night. That's me on the far left, beard and all. *Charles Hager collection.*

Uncle Columbus, who plucked me from the middle-of-nowhere, West Virginia, and introduced me to the Big Time, Chicago Heights. *Charles Hager collection.*

Columbus, second from right, in back, and my father, Robert, just to the left of him. *Charles Hager collection.*

Me with my 1975 El Dorado Cadillac. *Charles Hager collection.*

Me looking stylish in
1980. *Charles Hager collection.*

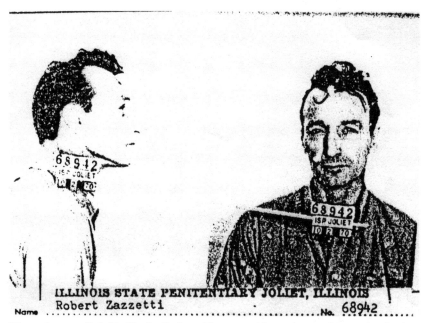

ILLINOIS STATE PENITENTIARY JOLIET, ILLINOIS
Name Robert Zazzetti   No. 68942

The infamous Bob Duff, aka Robert Zazzetti. He was in and out of jail a lot.
Charles Hager collection, from state prison archives.

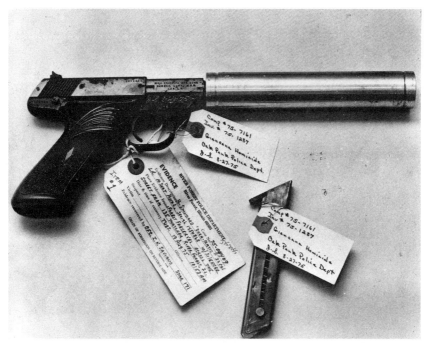

The gun that killed Sam Giancana, as tagged by the River Forest Police Department. I handled it many times. Inside the barrel is an insulated baffle with many small holes drilled into it. *John Binder collection.*

Two shots of Giancana, far right and second from left, with Anthony "Big Tuna" Accardo. *John Binder Collection.*

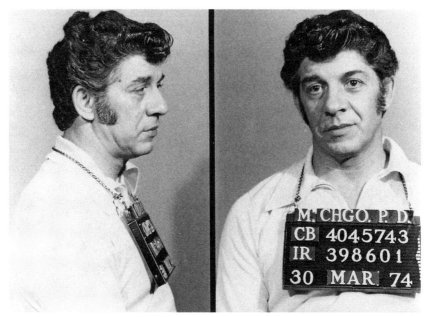

Al Tocco, long-serving boss of the South Side. *John Binder Collection.*

Johnny Roselli (sometimes spelled *Rosselli*), "Handsome Johnny," or "Johnny the Snake." He was older but still had the same eyes the night I chauffeured him. *John Binder Collection.*

The Dingess Tunnel, gateway from my life in Dingess to a rebirth in the larger world. Originally a railway tunnel, it's a single highway lane now over thirty-three hundred feet long, and has been the scene of much violence and many accidents. *Appalachian Magazine* called it "America's Bloodiest Tunnel." Some say it's haunted. *Courtesy Craig Hart.*

Claude "Big Daddy" Ellis, a legend in West Virginia politics who helped deliver the votes to JFK in the pivotal 1960 state primary election. *Courtesy Claudia Ellis.*

8. THE ROPES

While I knew I was on my way up in the mob, my rise wouldn't be as quick as I'd hoped. I was treated well, and most of the important guys seemed to like me. But I avoided many of the worst hands-on assignments and was glad to do so, as I was protected somewhat as a valuable driver and dependable odd-job man. Much like mine mules in the old days, those who get the very basic work done are treated better than middle management.

Once settled into the Heights, I began working directly for the top crew guys there as a chauffeur and gofer, gradually becoming more and more independent of Uncle Columbus, and I saw him much less often. The Outfit knew I wasn't grasping for a lot of power, so I wasn't offered the hard-core jobs. But I was a good driver. I came to know Chicago like I had been born there. Sometimes I drove for Pilotto, and many times for Tocco. I also found that everything you did was watched by the top guys in the Mob; it was eerie how much they knew, and how quickly they knew it. They realized that someday their lives and their freedom would rest on my loyalty and my ability to keep my mouth shut, so they watched me like a hawk before clueing me in on anything important.

Just as with cars, the Outfit always had chain-of-command "firebreaks," so the authorities could not grab a low-level member and get him to talk as they made their way up the Mob's leadership, arresting and sweating each guy as they went. A hood arrested in one operation could not lead the cops up the chain or across to other activities of the mob. A car stolen from the streets might be left and picked up three or four times before it was driven to the chop shop to be stripped of valuable components and parts.

I have to admit that the Mob was very disciplined in the way it drew you into illicit and illegal actions ever so gradually. It was like cooking a live frog slowly so he wouldn't jump out of the pot of hot water. You just raise the temperature a degree at a time until the unlucky frog is cooked. They cooked me nice and slow, but clearly I was moving up, getting more respect, and getting more responsibility, though they were careful to never give me more than I could handle. The bosses of the Mob weren't taking any chances despite the fact that they had grown to trust me. It helped that I came in as a kid under the close watch of Uncle Columbus, who had himself built up a long-time relationship with the Outfit.

For the next year or so, 1969 and '70, I was used mostly as a chauffeur and odd-job man and was doing nothing illegal. I continued to move cars with locked trunks from place to place and deliver unmarked packages, as I had done for Uncle Columbus, who I still went to see a couple of times a month. Because of the Mob's fear of a phone tap, I got my assignments by going to Vergie's Lounge, where the bartender might tell me, "Hey, Charley, show up here Friday night; we have a job for you." The Outfit always passed instructions and received reports one-on-one and face-to-face and operated as if every member's phone was tapped, and it probably was. But when it came to local law enforcement, the Outfit for all practical purposes owned the Chicago Heights police force. Al Pilotto's brother was the chief of police, staggering as that seems.

By 1970 I was working under the direction of Al Tocco, who had taken over all of Capone's old territory, from the garbage business to the numbers racket to nightclubs, loan sharking, prostitution, and protection; you name it, he made money from it. After I had done apprentice training with the Mob, I was used to keep people in line. Bluntly put, I was one of the organization's strongmen who made sure everyone paid their "street tax" to the Outfit, usually 10 percent of the business's gross income. I became known for using as little force and threat as possible to get the tax from everyone in my assigned area. I played one off the other as best I could. The tentacles of the Outfit stretched to virtually every vulnerable aspect of the Chicago Heights economy, from stripping down stolen cars to off-track betting, loan sharking, and illegal gambling. I had to find a niche there and started looking over the horses more and more closely.

Everyone in the Mob had a descriptive name. Mine was given me personally by Al Tocco, a huge honor. I was dubbed "Little Joe College" because I planned every move with extra care and I seldom made mistakes. Uncle Columbus had trained me well, and it was a good thing because mistakes were not acceptable under any circumstances. Remember, when I joined the Outfit I was a teenager, but by 1971 I was a street-savvy and disciplined twenty-one-year-old.

I moved up to working directly for Tocco in the years before the "chop shop wars," ruthless turf battles that cost dozens of lives, and I'm glad I missed them. A chop shop is a disguised or hidden garage, consisting of two or more bays. When a car is stolen in the chop shop's area, it is either brought there by the thief or, as in the case of the Outfit, by a chain of transfer guys. The chop shop pays the thief or the Organization for the stolen car and immediately goes about dismantling it, filing down the vehicle identification number, or VIN, usually breaking it down in about two hours, and then sending the parts out to potential buyers. The Outfit had an incredible distribution system for illicit car parts, a system that blanketed the entire United States and extended as far as Mexico and South America.

The chop shop wars broke out when rival gangs and organizations competed for the profits from each shop. The shops owned by Polish or Irish operators were pressured by the Outfit to pay their street tax, which, in effect, made the war an ethnic one between the Outfit's Italians and the Poles and Irish. Early in the chop-shop era, the Outfit was not concerned about them, but when Outfit bosses saw how lucrative the shops were, they made sure that every one of them in the Chicago area was paying the tax. They sent Jimmy "the Bomber" Cataura and four or five guys to take over any shops that were holding out. Although dozens of hits and bombings were made in the early and mid 1970s, Jimmy was not getting the job done. The Polish and Irish operators were giving as good as they got, and the death toll on both sides was rising fast. In the midseventies, the chop shop wars led to a massive slaughter, with literally dozens of competing players riddled with bullets and left dying in the streets. But the top fighters for the Outfit, guys like Billy Dauber, Nick D'Andrea, and the infamous Bob Duff, also known as Robert Zazzetti—about whom I'll say plenty more later—allegedly kept whacking the opposition well into the late seventies, when the turf battles really exploded and produced a river of blood. It was an all-out war between the rival gangs, but events conspired to prevent my being there during that era, and that's why I'm alive today.

Even in my time there, the gangs that fought it out around me seemed to be everywhere. I recall a specific incident in 1972, a Mob hit, resulting directly from those wars. Purely by chance I was there: August 8, just before

10 A.M., according to the newspaper account,[1] after I got off the third shift at DeSoto Chemicals I pulled into Malizia's gas station on Route 30. There, pumping gas into his car, was a guy who turned out to be Guido Fidanzi, accused of stealing three or four hundred cars and planning to testify against the Outfit. After Fidanzi hung up the pump and headed for the men's room, three guys with handkerchiefs over their faces pulled up in a gold Cadillac and ran after him. "Oh, shit," I thought to myself; "this is not good."

By then I had learned not to look too closely at things I shouldn't see, but some things happen so quickly the self-protective part of the brain has no time to overrule the natural instinct to pay close attention. One set of eyes visible over the handkerchiefs was unmistakable: deep, clear, and cold eyes I would later recognize as Bob Duff's.

And the situation *wasn't* good, certainly not for Fidanzi, because the three hoods snatched guns from under their coats and started pumping rounds into that men's room door. After many rounds they kicked it open and fired a half-dozen rounds into what I assume was already the corpse of Fidanzi. I didn't wait to see anything more. I put the nozzle back in the pump, jumped in my car, hit the gas pedal, and hightailed it out of there. I read about the hit the next day in the paper.

POKER WAS A big source of income for the Mob as well as a major source of socializing and entertainment. As I was making my bones in the Outfit, besides moving cars with locked trunks around, I'd also help with the supervision and operation of poker games. One guy I supported in a Mob-run poker game was Frank D'Andrea, Nick's brother, who ran one of the better-known high-stakes games. He weighed 350 or 400 pounds and didn't like to move much, so he'd send me around the table to take the Outfit's cut.

In the Heights, every little joint had its own card game, sometimes in a back room, sometimes upstairs, sometimes during the day but normally after hours. There were games that you knew would attract big players, where the stakes started out high and stayed high. Other games were normally low-stake or penny-ante games that had limits on the bets. And then there were games that started small and all of a sudden caught fire and became high-stakes. Some of the joints had a standard time and place for a game to start, and either five- or seven-card stud was played, depending on the number of players. Once a game started, you were in the room until it was over so that nobody could call the cops. It could last twenty or thirty hours. No other game was played. I played cards but soon found out that it was not my game, so I began to focus almost exclusively on horse racing.

One of the most frequented joints with high-stakes games was the Vagabond Lounge, where the big games were played in the rooms above the bar. There were plenty of rooms to pick from, and there was also a room in the back of the adjacent liquor store, but the location of games was changed constantly to avoid a raid. There would never be a game in any one place two days in a row. Now, none of these guys were afraid of the local cops, because the police protected the games and often played in them. But we couldn't control the Illinois state vice squads. These were special ATF units formed to make a couple dozen raids and then disband. The ATF leaders would never tell the local cops about any upcoming raid, because they knew the word would be out on the street in a heartbeat.

I often asked myself, "Why in the hell would some of these guys keep playing games where the house not only took an automatic cut but would fix the game any way they could?" Well, the answer is that they were stupid. They were just stupid. Some of these guys who got hooked by the Mob were just like an alcoholic whose jar of moonshine has a scorpion on its lid. The drinker is going to get stung because he has to have that drink. Not only that, the cardplayers compounded their stupidity by getting in the juice (street loans) lines to borrow money from the Mob at 100 percent interest. They never got out of debt, and if they even thought of weaseling out of it they were subject to being, at best, beaten up or, at worst, killed. Of course, the Mob would accept stolen goods as payment. They didn't care. But they would never allow the debtor credit for anywhere near its actual value. The unlucky debtor might get strung along or allowed to do work for the interest, but they never got free. Never.

Without question, anything that could be rigged or fixed by the Outfit was rigged or fixed. There were peepholes in the ceiling of many card rooms, with wires connected to specific seats through which the players were told when they had the winning hand and could bet anything they wanted or when they had a losing hand and needed to fold.

The Outfit also controlled and profited from loan sharking and prostitution in bars and brothels throughout their area of operation. But the leadership of the Outfit wanted members to have a legitimate job as a cover, which I always did, starting off with Sears Roebuck. Later I leased a farm of about ten acres north of Route 57, just a half mile or so from my other lease, on the Ralph Daum farm. Nearby was an Amoco gas station for sale on a pretty good road, so I did a little checking around and put a bid on it. The price on the station was already reasonable, but because the owner was going to Florida and wanted to get out of there fast, I put in a low bid and the owner took it. From then on I personally opened up the station almost every morning and was there most of the hours it was open. In the first years after buying the station I worked ten or twelve hours a day, and many days I'd wind up grabbing an hour or two of sleep in my office in the back of the place.

All this was good for my reputation with the mob, because the Outfit wanted you to have a family and an honest business. I was building not only a good reputation inside the organization but also the kind of life outside the organization they wanted to see. Remember, a tax evasion charge eventually brought down Capone. I recall Columbus saying very seriously to me, "You gotta keep good books. Most guys in the Outfit who go to jail go for tax evasion and cooking the books. Whatever books you're going to submit to the IRS have to be spot-on and honest. If the feds find a guy they think is doing illegal stuff, the first thing they do is check his taxes. If they can't get their target for nothin' else, they get 'em for tax evasion." Many mobsters besides Capone went to jail for violating tax laws. There is no statute of limitation on taxes owed, so I never had a large amount of money in the house. My gas station and harness-racing records and earnings were kept in the bank, because I knew that if the Feds were after you for anything, the first thing they would do was get a warrant and search every nook and cranny of your house. The second place they'd go was your bank to audit your books and money. The IRS did everything in the world to find something wrong with my books, but they never could, because all my records were squeaky clean. I kept my businesses thoroughly honest and precisely accounted for. As a matter of fact, I had my accountant review and sign off on all my books and records at the end of every month.

Any money to me from the Mob was always in cash, which I kept either in my pocket or, as I had learned in my West Virginia upbringing, in several glass-topped Mason jars, buried where no one would find them. Call me a hillbilly, but a carefully buried Mason jar would never be found and could last a hundred years. This practice would eventually pay off, literally, just a few years later.

Just as in a legitimate bar business, Uncle Columbus also knew he had to watch out for everything to keep the hangers-on from robbing him blind. It was a game of economic survival. He taught me to do the same, so we always had two pairs of eyes watching. He also taught me to think out every move I was to make and to weigh the consequences. I learned to operate with a cool but careful detachment, just like him. Those early years with Uncle Columbus provided an incredible experience in managing power and in conducting both legal and illegal business, experiences that have served me all my life.

9. YOU CAN'T WIN, YOU CAN'T BREAK EVEN, YOU CAN'T EVEN LEAVE THE GAME

*B*esides rigging card games, the Mob also fixed trotting races, which became my specialty as I moved up. I first became a horse racing fan when I started working on the Outfit's side of the sport in 1968. In that era harness racing was totally corrupt, but I fell in love with it, and by 1972 I kept trotting horses on the small farm near my Amoco station, winding up with seven trotters with good bloodlines. From then on, I raced my horses, drove horses, ate, slept, and loved horses. I brought my experience from our Dingess farm to the care and feeding of my harness horses, since I had spent fourteen years working, feeding, training, harnessing, watering, and caring for horses at home when I was growing up. (To my regret, I paid more attention to my horses then than I did to my kids.) My sister-in-law's husband was a top trotting-horse driver, which gave a real edge to my horse operations for both the Outfit and myself. My wife at that time loved the races, and we'd often go together, so harness racing was both an increasing source of income and a key component of Hager entertainment. Eventually, I became the Outfit's primary harness operator, bettor, and racing guru for all their trotting-horse operations.

I'm making no accusations about horse or harness racing in America today, but I can say with total authority and much hands-on experience that, back then, harness racing in the greater Chicago area was as crooked as a dog's hind leg. Everyone involved in the races, other than the crowd who just watched and bet on them, was to some degree crooked. Everyone in the know traded information, and every race was fixed to some extent. But by Syndicate standards, harness racing was nonviolent. I think one of the reasons I am still alive today is that I came to specialize in racing operations rather than the wet work of shooting and killing for the Outfit.

Strangely enough, the first horse I bought and owned was registered to a well-known mobster in the Syndicate, a guy who was part of the Twenty-Sixth Street Crew, Joe Lavolsi. That horse ran his first race for me under

Lavolsi's name before I could get it registered in my own name. Joe didn't actually own the horse; it was owned by another hood who had been in trouble with the law and, therefore, as a felon, could not register a racehorse.

Now, I knew it would be not only a challenge but a longshot for a young West Virginia country boy to work his way into the "in crowd" at a northern Illinois racetrack where there was big money to be made. But I did have some advantages. I was young and fairly new to the game at the track and so was able to fly under the radar for a while. When I got the first of my seven racehorses, I combined my childhood love and respect for horses with my love for the racetrack, because the track was always good to me. The Outfit learned to respect my instincts for horses, and that regard soon extended to betting. I didn't always win. Nobody does, but more often than not when I'd put a ten-dollar bet down, I'd bring home $1,200. It wasn't long after acquiring more horses and keeping some of them at the track that I became a well-known insider at Balmoral Racetrack in Crete, Illinois.

Although I was not a licensed driver, I could train offtrack or at one of the state fairs and even drove some races there. There is nothing more challenging and thrilling than driving a nine-hundred-pound, incredibly disciplined horse that is trained to race against other horses as fast as it can at either a trotting or a pacing gait, without once breaking into a gallop. Driving a trotting or pacing horse is an in-the-dirt thrill because the driver is sitting two feet off the ground on a two-wheeled cart called a sulky, which is only a foot from the horse's back hooves and positioned so that the driver's eyes are looking up at the horse's rear. So, for the entire race, you have to look around the horse to see what is ahead, and if the track is wet, you're looking through mud-splashed goggles. It's like standing in the trunk of a race car, driving by ropes hitched to the steering wheel while running the entire race in second gear.

Thoroughbred racing may be the sport of kings, but harness racing was the sport of the Outfit then. It seems like the lessons that Uncle Columbus drummed into my head verbally, and drove home even more powerfully by example, served me well in my role at the track. Both as a business enterprise and as entertainment, harness racing was big in the life of the Syndicate, and most members of the Outfit, upper and lower, even the street hoods, were involved in some way in harness racing. If there was a horse race and someone on the street had a wad of cash in his pocket to put a bet down, it would be put down. If there was a card game or a horse race, somebody was going to call the bets. Street arguments by lowly hoods about which horse was better would turn into a wad of cash literally being thrown down on the sidewalk. Making flamboyant bets on a race was one way a small-time hood could get known as an up-and-comer, and it was a way to show he had balls. Sometimes as foolish as they were brash, bettors would throw a whole bundle of cash out there to prove they were the man! As often as not the guy lost it all and maybe the week's food for his family. Actually, in most bets, two guys had to make the bet: the one who threw the money down on a three-horse race saying that one horse would win and another guy to call the bet, saying another horse would win. Almost every time a bet changed hands on the streets of Chicago Heights, the Mob took a hunk of it.

At the other end of the betting chain, there were dozens of ways the Syndicate could put the fix on a race's outcome, including cooperation among the jockeys to win, place, show, or fade. Each track had its gathering of influential insiders who got exclusive information, but for many of the tracks around the Heights, the Outfit had the farthest reach and the greatest influence. Now, most of the race officials and track vets were pretty straight, but that didn't keep the insiders from getting around them.

So even though I was young, the Mob quickly figured that I had become as close to a technical and operational expert on harness racing as they had. I was especially valuable in making large bets for the Mob. From time to time, the top people in the Mob wanted to place a large bet, probably anywhere from $4,000 to $7,500, which was big money in those days but not big enough to impact the odds for betting on the horse. Some of these big bets might come from one of the upper-echelon bosses. Or it might come from a street bookie who had to accept the bet but did not want to accept the downside risk of a $5,000 bet that at ten-to-one might take $50,000 out of his pocket. Only a racetrack could accept that kind of one-time downside risk.

About ten to fifteen times a month I was called in by one of the bosses and told something like, "Charley, here's five thousand dollars. I want you to bet it on King George to win. Got that?"

"Got it," I answered. I never placed a bet at the window myself. I'd always find some track bum or a local wino or some poor sap who was in debt to the Mob and needed to pay off a loan or do the Mob a favor. I had a good reason for making the Mob's bets that way: when you placed a large bet at the ticket window and won, the winnings were registered with the IRS and 20 percent was taken off the top right at the window and sent to the IRS.

If I had personally gone to the window with the Mob's bets, as well as my own, my accumulated track earnings would earn me a staggering tax bill. But the wino with a negative net worth and no income would probably pay no taxes on his registered winnings, if he filed at all. I'd find someone in the Heights who we knew was OK, take him to the track, and use him to make the bet. Once he had my client's money in his pocket I watched him like a hawk until he placed the bet and got the track ticket. If the horse won, he got the winnings. Then I would quietly find an obscure place to take the winnings from him and give him a hundred or so for his trouble. Sometimes, after a winning bet had been picked up, I'd tell the guy, "Come on, I'll give you a ride to the Heights," and then take the money as I dropped him off. Even the bookies on the street would take to the track any large bet they were given. They were not going to turn a bet down, but they weren't going to bankroll that large a bet because it was too much risk. Bookies are like banks: they like lots of small amounts, not one large one.

The Mob didn't pay me for making a bet for them. My payment came from the fact that, when a fix was on, I was let in on it and was able to place my own legit bet on a horse with a probability of winning that was far better than average. That information proved pretty lucrative, because you wouldn't believe how many races in northern Illinois were fixed. How could that happen when the racing commission is watching everything? Easy. You could, for example, flood the field: the "fixer" would wait until he found a race with a field of cheap horses, bought for $1,000, $1,500, or anything below $5,000. Then he would sneak into that race a horse that was not well known to racing officials but had a pretty good record. You could get the word on a horse from the drivers or track vets who knew what that horse was capable of doing. In addition, we'd carefully look for a horse that was trained away from the track and was in really good shape. We'd get that horse in a race to give us the highest odds. Our "snuck-in" horse might be assigned odds of fifteen to one, twenty to one, or even twenty-five to one.

Then there's boxing a high-odds horse, that is, making deals with some of the others to box out, or force to the outside, any challengers so they had to run a longer race. Once most of the horses were forced to the outside, the cooperating drivers let our favored horse through on the inside. Racing is counted in seconds, and just that difference in race positions will give an inside horse a big advantage. But this kind of fix was not perfect. You try to keep your favored horse out of harm's way, and lots of people will be helping you, but, again, anything can happen. Also, though I hated it, sometimes the food of a favored horse was doctored. Or a horse was drugged with something called "apple morphine." A fixer would choose a horse that was highly favored to win out of the paddock, find a blind spot on the path, and hit the horse on the neck with a hidden syringeful, slowing him down. The bought-off drivers would steer the preferred horse to the win.

Not only did I have three years of as-good-as-it-gets apprenticeship in smart crime operations with Uncle Columbus; I also carried with me the instincts of a poor country farm kid. I didn't have much, but if I got something, I'd protect the hell out of it. Beyond a natural understanding of horses and horse racing, the caution and judgment I learned from the poverty of a small farm and working for my Uncle Columbus built up discretion in me. I didn't bet money I didn't have, and when I did bet, it wasn't on instinct but on analysis of every condition and factor about the horse, the weather, and the track. Thus, at twenty-five, I had both a legit job and a street job, and both taught me well. Though I have only a ninth-grade formal education, I'd put my street education with the Heights bosses, underbosses, and street players up against anyone's.

During the last years of my horse-racing life, I was accepted and welcomed everywhere at my home track, from all the clubs and bars to the paddocks. I was one of a few who could go anywhere at any time, night or day, because I was recognized but also because I was an owner. I had a horse-racing license, just like a driver's license, and I did conduct some shady operations. If you got caught doing anything suspicious the authorities could and would take your license. You never knew when you were going to be investigated. Tocco and Pilotto constantly had a camera on them. And you never knew about the IRS; they might be coming after someone else but wind up investigating you to get to them. So whenever I put the fix on a race, which was always at the request of the Mob, I was careful not to leave any provable trace of my illicit actions.

From the time I joined the Mob in the late sixties, until the fateful events of 1975, it was an exciting life, and the fact that I came to specialize in trotting race operations and race fixing made it especially great because I was spending more and more time at the track betting my money and the Mob's money and racing my own pacing horses. There were a few bumps along the way but nothing I couldn't handle.

I worked hard, but it wasn't all work. I had met a young woman and married her in 1968. I did my best to shield her from my activities, with limited success; for reasons that will become clear, I won't go into detail about our relationship, but during my apprentice years with the Outfit, I kept my private life aboveboard and as separate from my Mob life as possible. I soon had a growing family, four kids born in quick succession. When I wasn't running the service station or doing jobs for the Mob, I was home. Life was good.

10. MR. LUCKY

Roland Vance was also from a large family that lived in and around Logan, and like me he went back and forth between there and Chicago. There seemed to be a pipeline sending young, ambitious men from Logan into Chicago, Detroit, and Cleveland. Just as with a regular job, with many miners relocating for factory work in the north or millwork in the south when the mining industry went into one of its cyclical busts, we had to leave West Virginia for any shot at a future.

Vance and I both ran with some tough characters, Spry among them, but Roland had a special and well-earned reputation as a loose cannon. He started young, his tough early life propelling him first to burglary and then to cold-blooded murder. Like many of the guys on the streets of the Heights, he had some special quirks that might have made him endearing were he someone's peaceful, law-abiding friend or family member. In Vance's case it was puzzles. He was in and out of prison so often he had plenty of time to develop a talent for solving various kinds of puzzles, even winning $500 in a newspaper contest while he was in the Logan County jail in 1973.[1] The story hit the Associated Press wires, and a lot of papers picked it up. There was plenty of irony to go around. "If His Luck Holds . . ." read the headline. Vance said that "if his luck is as good with the Parole Board," he wanted to start a new life by returning to a "former job in Chicago." Outfit work was always waiting for someone like him. He was good with guns, that's all. Not bright. As much of a screwup as he could be, and as much poor judgment as he could show, Vance had a special relationship with the cops, both in Logan and in Chicago Heights. Just from the paper trail of his criminal activity—burglary, parole violations, and an indictment for his role in a homicide in late 1973—you'd think the authorities would have thrown Vance under the jail. But in most instances he found some way around the charges or served only a fraction of the time you'd think a habitual offender should. I admit I know much of this about Vance because I was there, literally.

I spent time in that same jail in Logan with Vance when I was younger and had been warned to stay away from him by the local cop who was my ears to the outside.

Yet, as with Vance and a lot of the other guys, they weren't comic-book gangsters. Each seemed to have some odd quirk of normalcy, whether it was being a whiz at puzzles or making a success at a legitimate business and not needing any ill-gotten gains but still living that life. For what? I often wondered. If you had plenty to live on, was it just the thrill of having that kind of life-and-death power that a made man carries with him everywhere?

Early in 1975, when I was twenty-five, I was introduced by Al Tocco and Nick D'Andrea to Bob Duff. That meeting would change my life and mark the beginning of the end of my time in the Outfit. Duff was brought back from the Ozarks to become one of the Outfit's most dangerous and, I found out later, off-kilter hit men. His quirk—go figure—was his talent as a painter.[2]

Duff was sixteen years older than I and had grown up with my mentor in the Outfit, Nick D'Andrea, in a neighborhood called "Hungry Hill" outside Chicago. It got that name during the Depression because so many people there were so poor and so hungry. Nick told me that some of the kids from there were called "two-tomato" children because that's all they had for lunch.

I knew Duff was a tough customer, and it was understood among our crew that he was of great value to the Outfit as among the best of its hitmen. As soon as we met I began trying to recall where I'd seen those cold-steel eyes. It took me a while. I pondered that mystery until we were forced to go on a job together, then remembered their cold stare as their owner prepared to pump bullet after bullet into Fidanzi at the gas station men's room. I kept my distance from Duff as best I could, but it seemed like he was hanging around more and more, and obviously was a go-to guy for D'Andrea. I had no choice but to get to know him, and on our assignments I spent more time than I cared to with him. Duff/Zazzetti had a long and "illustrious" career before I got to know him, including a 1961 conviction for burglary,[3] being a suspect (and probably guilty) in a 1963 series of drugstore burglaries during which drugs and narcotics were taken,[4] a 1963 perjury indictment,[5] a 1968 motel theft in Carbondale, Illinois, and more. He was an expert at picking locks. He never did much time; despite his extracurricular activities he was apparently too valuable to the Outfit. He was paroled from Joliet for a 1968 Ogle, Illinois, service station burglary,[6] and when he was found guilty of a 1970 weapons charge and sentenced to four to eight years, he served less than two. The cops had plenty of opportunities to send him away for a long time but didn't, as the Outfit protected him too well.[7]

I was pretty good at sizing people up, but Duff was a tough nut to crack. I knew he had plenty of very chancy assignments, and though he was ruthlessly efficient about the actual jobs, he could be impulsive when he was on his own. Duff's character shows through clearly in his attempted murder of a guy named Charles Krask. Duff had killed or tried to kill, to my personal knowledge, three people in just four months. The second attempt of those three was Krask. In the attempted Krask hit, Duff and his accomplice pumped a few rounds into the 350-pound Krask and blew him down the basement stairs of his home. But the tenacious Krask lived to testify against Duff. The newspaper accounts and abstract of Duff's trial describe what happened. The abstract of Duff/Zazzetti's trial read,

> Charles Krask testified that about 1 A.M., July 2, 1975, he was shot in the stomach while standing at the back door of his house. Earlier, on the evening of July 1, 1975, Krask and a woman friend had several drinks at the Vagabond Lounge in Chicago Heights, Illinois, where Krask argued with the defendant, who he knew by the name of Bob Duff. An argument started, according to Krask, after he accidentally bumped into the defendant. Krask and his friend left the bar, and went home.
>
> Sometime near 1 A.M., the couple was awakened by a pounding noise. Krask got up, checked the living room and then went to the rear of his house. He flicked on the outside lights which illuminated the backyard because the yard without lights was very dark.
>
> Krask testified that he saw two men in the backyard, about 10 feet away, looking at him and approaching the house with metal objects in their hands. Krask watched them for about three or four seconds, saw flashes, heard a report and was struck by something which caused him to fall down the basement stairs. He lay in the basement in pain and bleeding for several minutes before struggling up the stairs to the kitchen. His friend came into the kitchen and, at Krask's request, called the police. She testified at trial, corroborating Krask's description of the evening.[8]

Nick D'Andrea came to my house and asked me if I had been with Duff the night before. I told him the truth: I had not. The police arrested Duff at 1:30 the same morning near the Vagabond Lounge in a car driven by Joe Barrett, the owner of the car. During the arrest a spent shell casing was found in the car, and a ballistics investigation proved that the casing had been expelled from the same weapon used to shoot Krask. The Mob tried to cover for Duff and Barrett by having Barrett's friend Jacqueline Munro and Barrett's brother, James Watkins, testify that Duff was at the Vagabond Lounge from midnight to 1:30 A.M. on the night of the shooting. To no avail. Duff was convicted and sentenced to ten to thirty years in prison, but whatever the decision of the court, I know for a fact that Duff spent only two years in prison and was released. Typical for the Outfit, murders went unsolved; witnesses "forgot" what they saw. In the 1990s dozens of Cook County judges were indicted, as the feds helped clean things up, but back in my day, judges, lawyers, court clerks, bailiffs, you name it, they had their hands out and you could get done just about anything you wanted to. (Nick D'Andrea allegedly had friends in the Heights police department, one of whom apparently bribed a clerk to switch Nick's booking mug shot with his brother Mario's to throw off an investigation. The switch led to a circus when Nick's killer, Jimmy Marcello, was finally tried; the jury deadlocked, and who knows if it was compromised, but the judge found Marcello guilty anyway and sentenced him to life.[9] Nick Calabrese, in the Family Secrets trial,[10] looked at the photo of Mario and identified it as Nick D'Andrea, testimony that was dramatically contradicted by Nick's girlfriend.[11]) But that cleanup came long after my time in the Heights. During my era there, if the evidence was too overwhelming to buy off the cops or the judge, connected guys rarely served more than a token sentence. And they were protected while inside and had their old job waiting for them when they got out.

Duff's main competition in the killing department was Billy Dauber. Dauber was ruthless as hell; he seemed to take pleasure in his job. Dauber's father had worked for Al Capone as a hit man, and in 1980 Dauber, who had become a major enforcer for the Outfit in the chop shop wars, was hit himself, along with his wife, hours after he made the mistake of testifying.[12] This ended the short but sordid career of Dauber, who had killed more than twenty people. Duff probably killed an equal number and deserved "credit" for many attributed, to this day, to Dauber.

The lives of Spry, Duff, and Vance would intersect with my own, and I would not only play an unwitting role in one of their deaths but also come close to killing another. The state, via a fellow inmate, would take care of the third. It all revolved around a cheap gun. Spry knew Vance better than

I did. Spry had won a .22 pistol from Vance in a poker game in Logan. The gun was a High Standard Duromatic, and the normally four-inch barrel had been cut down and fitted with a homemade silencer, maybe made from a lawnmower muffler, with numerous holes drilled into the silencer barrel and some kind of baffles stuffed inside. The .22 was a favored tool for the Outfit's hit men—reliable, reasonably cheap, and capable of doing great harm with a single bullet, if you didn't want to go to the trouble of a larger caliber or sawed-off shotgun. According to both Duff and Spry, I later learned, the pistol had been given to Vance by two Chicago cops who were working for the Outfit. Neither Duff nor Spry knew (or at least didn't tell me) who Vance was supposed to hit with it, but in any event Vance didn't follow through on the job. Spry told me that Vance turned the gun on the two cops instead, though I've never been able to verify that, as I can't find any record of two Chicago cops being killed with a handgun on about the same day in what would have been around February 1975. When Vance returned to Logan after another run-in with the law, he was clearly desperate for money and got cleaned out by Spry in a poker game at Dick's club in Dingess. Poker games in Logan or Dingess were no more straight, I'm sure, than those in Chicago, though in this case I can't vouch for anything but Vance's thick-headedness.

I see that gun in my mind as clearly as I did the day I first handled it. Sure, it was just a cheap gun, maybe worth a hundred dollars at best, but with the silencer in place it was worth a good chunk of Vance's $1,500 debt to Spry. The police would eventually find the gun and say it originally came from Florida. Maybe that's true; I have no way of knowing. Guns flowed into Chicago from everywhere. But how did the .22 make its way to little Logan County, West Virginia, to begin with? I pieced the story together. Vance had been jailed, along with two other people, for the murder of a man named Larry Jarrett. The Jarrett homicide charge went away when one of his accomplices turned out to be an unreliable witness. Earlier Logan County charges were similarly dissolved. I'm certain that on his release from jail Vance, needing money and glad to leave Chicago for a while, headed back to Logan. That's when he thought, wrongly, he could raise some money in a poker game; instead he dug himself in deeper.

Vance hatched another ill-conceived plan: he needed a quick score so he decided to rob a Logan gun shop and unload the guns quickly. If need be he could take the guns back to Chicago, where they would be easily sold. On February 20 he and two brothers, James and Donald Marcum, broke into the Baisden Brothers store in Logan and stole sixteen guns plus ammunition. Vance tried to sell the guns at the Lucky Star Club but had no takers. The trio spent the night at Vance's half-brother's house and the next day loaded the guns into a car, inexplicably leaving three of them behind. The store owner shortly identified them as three of the stolen guns. The Marcums were arrested and took the state police to Vance's half-brother's house. A few days later Vance, no genius, offered to sell two guns to one of the Baisden brothers, who contacted the police. Vance was picked up and shortly thereafter sentenced to life as a habitual criminal.[13] His luck had run out—but not before he delivered that little .22 into the hands of Dick Spry in that fateful poker game.

11. A PUNK IN THE TRUNK

*D*espite my uneasiness around Duff, life was good for me. I had a family, a small business, and my own harness racing license. Life was especially sweet compared to my early childhood and to the lives of the kids who could not escape Dingess.

BY THE SPRING of 1975 I was busy with my horses and legitimate business but still needed to be available when Nick D'Andrea wanted me to do something. Periodically, I checked in at the Vagabond Lounge, Vergie's, or the Liberty Restaurant and often would find I had a mission for that night. It might be a pickup or a meet with a couple of other guys to put some muscle on a store owner who wasn't paying his "taxes." I'd make two or three such missions a week, still working with my horses at all other times.

One day in April of 1975 I was at Vergie's and was sent to the Vagabond Lounge to talk to Joe Barrett and wait for Duff to bring money from someplace in Manteno, Illinois. An hour or two and a couple of beers later, no Bob. I was sitting with Nick, Barrett, and Al Tocco in a back booth of the lounge, and after a while Joe said, "Where the hell is Duff?" The rest of us gave him a blank stare. Joe said, "He was out on a run, and he ain't come back." Then Tocco said, "I'm gonna check. Be right back." A couple of minutes later, Tocco came back to our booth with a worried look on his face. "Duff made the pickup an hour and a half ago. He should have been here twenty minutes ago. Go find him." Joe sent me and several guys from the bar to Duff's pickup point. He gave us the make and model of Bob's car and the routes he could have taken back to the Lounge and assigned each of us a different route to check out.

I didn't have to be told twice. I barreled out of the Vagabond, ran to my car, and headed up Illinois Route 1 and then to Beecher Highway, my assigned route. As I broke out of the Heights and into the more rural areas of cornfields with cinder roads between, I looked left and right for Duff's car. The first time I ran my assigned route, I ran it pretty quickly but didn't see Duff. When I turned around and headed back, I made it more slowly and took a longer look up each side road and cinder trail. Still nothing.

I turned around again, and took a long stare down each side road and cinder trail until I was sure there was nothing unusual along it. Eventually, I was looking around the town of Beecher, Illinois, an area near Crete. I had been looking there for twenty minutes, driving up and down the paved road and peering down each side road, and after rounding one curve I slowed down and looked down the next cinder trail between two cornfields. About 250 feet from the main road I saw a brown Buick with smoke billowing out of the front seat and a black sedan pulling away. "Shit," I said to myself, "that can't be Bob, can it?" I slammed the car in reverse. I shoved the gearshift back into drive, shot forward, spun an instant right, and skidded down the cinder trail. My headlights picked up the burning car. Instantly, I knew it was Bob's, and with that came the realization that he was in trouble. I could also see that the black sedan pulling away from Bob's car was heading straight toward me. I swerved to avoid it and in the dark I couldn't get a good look inside. It sped away, and I continued toward Bob as fast as I could.

I slid my car to a stop, but not too close to Bob's, in case his car blew up. I jumped out of the car and covered the fifteen yards to Bob's car as fast as I could, running and shouting for Bob at every step. As I got closer, I saw that flames were spreading through the cabin. Looking into the smoky interior of the car, I saw no sign of Bob, but I couldn't see below the seats. I stopped yelling for Bob for a second and waited for a response, and immediately heard banging and muffled screams coming from the trunk. I knew it had to be Bob, and I also knew I didn't have much time.

I ran back to the trunk of my car, fumbled my key into the trunk lock, and flipped it open. I always kept a sawed-off twelve-gauge shotgun there and pulled it out. Running back to Bob's car, I clicked off the safety, held the gun down with the muzzle in the trunk lock, and fired. The lock blew off and the trunk popped up about a foot. I tried to push the trunk lid the rest of the way up with my arm, but it was stuck. I stooped down under the trunk lid, got my legs and shoulder under me, and pushed up. The hinges gave way with a groan, and I was able to push the trunk the rest of the way open. I looked down into the trunk where Bob lay, hands and feet wrapped with duct tape, writhing in pain and beaten to crap, with knife cuts on his arms and one big gash about five inches long down his leg.

Smelling the gasoline and scared of the car blowing up, I quickly reached into the trunk, grabbed Bob by his leather jacket, hauled him up and over the edge, and flopped him on the ground. He screamed in pain when he hit the ground, but I didn't wait to cut him loose. I dragged him about twenty feet down the gravel road away from the car, which was by now burning in earnest. Bob was lucky that the hoods who messed him up had left the windows and the doors closed, so the fire was slow in catching. Had they left them open, the car would have exploded before I found Duff.

After I got the tape off his arms and legs, I unfastened his belt, yanked it from his pants, and used it as a tourniquet around his leg. The belt wouldn't tighten enough to stop the flow of blood, but I managed to fasten it with one hand and keep it in place with a hunk of the duct tape that had been on his wrist. All the while I kept watch for the black sedan to return. No one else knew where I was, and whoever was in the car might return to finish off both of us.

Bob was still screaming in pain as I ran to get my car and backed it up to where he lay writhing. "Man," I said, "I got to get you to a hospital; you look bad."

"No! No way. No hospital!" he screamed.

"You're crazy, man, you gotta get a doc. You've been cut up. Who did this?" I asked. He refused to say. "Get me the hell to the Vagabond," he said through the pain. "Now."

"You need a doctor; nobody can help you at the lounge," I yelled back.

"You heard me," he yelled. "Get me to the lounge!"

"Who messed you up?" I yelled at him.

"Never mind that; get me to the damn lounge."

"OK," I said, "It's your funeral." I hefted him into my backseat and half laid, half pushed him into the car.

By this time, Bob's car was completely engulfed, and I saw the flames in my rearview mirror as I picked up speed down the cinder road toward the main road. After another hundred feet, I heard a muffled explosion and saw it blazing in the rearview.

All the way back to the lounge I heard Bob moaning, and every three or four moans he would cry out in pain, "It's killin' me."

Once on the main road I floored it and headed toward the lounge. I looked down at the speedometer and saw it passing eighty, but I had to chance getting picked up by the cops because I thought Bob could be dying, even though his groans told me he was still very much alive. Halfway back to the lounge he quieted down for a minute, and I tried to ask him again, "Bob, who messed you up like this?"

He let out another loud moan, and I knew that even if he was certain of dying he wouldn't tell me who had done it.

I finally got to the lounge and came to a screeching halt in front of the lounge door. I jumped out of the driver's seat, yanked the front door open by its brass handle, and ran into the lounge bar. Just inside I saw Joe Barrett standing by the bar. "Bob's out in my car! He's been cut up and beaten up; help me get him in!" Barrett, Tocco, and two other guys followed me out. The four of us carried him into the lounge. He was still bleeding, but the tourniquet on his leg had stopped the worst of it.

We hauled Bob back into the kitchen of the bar and laid him out on a long steel-topped table. Joe went upstairs and brought back a guy named Dr. Panio, who cut the clothes off Bob and began sewing up the bigger gashes. Bob continued yelling and cursing while sucking down the scotch we were pouring into him for the pain. Between Bob's cries Tocco yelled down at him, "Duff, who messed you up like this?" "Some guys I used to know in the Ozarks," he screamed back. "They're dead; they just don't know it."

As Dr. Panio continued to work on Duff and the alcohol kicked in, Duff quieted down a bit, but it was obvious he was still in a lot of pain. Regardless, he still wouldn't go to a hospital. He kept saying, "They're dead; they just don't know it. Dead, but don't know it. They're going to die and die hard." Duff was as tough as they come, and I knew he was capable of anything.

Four days later, Joe Barrett told me that Bob needed a place to cool off, to lay low until they got this thing figured out. Joe said, "Charley, you got a place you aren't using?" I swallowed hard. I did own a small rental house. I didn't let on but I had my reservations about putting Duff up. "Yeah," I said. "Bob can have it." After all, this was Joe and Nick asking. No refusal, right?

It took Bob a couple of weeks to recover from his wounds. Meanwhile everyone was going crazy trying to figure out what had happened. I gradually got the story out of Bob. He had been a bouncer down in the Ozarks working for a guy named Don Hammond, who used to own a joint called the Roaring '20s in Chicago Heights. Back in the 1960s Don had been booted out of town by a bunch of people in the Heights because he had allegedly stolen thousands of dollars from people there and cracked a lot of heads, at least according to Duff.

Hammond and Duff had been working together in Quincy, Illinois, running cathouses, when Bob was pulled back to the Heights by Al Tocco in early 1975, probably to do some hits in the Chicago area because the chop shop wars were heating up. Hammond tipped the boys in Quincy that Bob was normally carrying a lot of money from one place to another. We didn't have the foggiest idea why Hammond or his buddies decided to rob Duff, but whatever genius thought that one up made a big mistake.

When he had recovered well enough from his wounds, Duff disappeared for a while, presumably returning to the Ozarks to settle accounts there. When he got back, Tocco, Nick D'Andrea, Duff and I met at the Vagabond in one of the upstairs rooms as a kind of homecoming for Duff, but I didn't know going in it was also a celebration for me. We all had a few drinks, and Tocco made a little speech:

"Listen up, assholes. We're all glad to have Bob Duff back after his little visit to the Ozarks, to tell the guys who screwed him up and left him in a burning car to die how much he appreciated their visit. But, I gotta say that Duff would not be here tonight if Little Joe College had not found him and pulled him from the trunk of a burning car after he had been beaten and cut up with a knife. Some of you guys saw how messed up Duff was when they brought him into the lounge.

"So I want you guys, and everyone in the Outfit, to know that while Little Joe College ain't no paisano, he's still a good friend of the Outfit. So, here's to Little Joe, and all you mothers shake his hand and welcome him into the Outfit." Now, I couldn't be "made" in the typical Mob sense because I wasn't Italian (though I understand that Jimmy Marcello, who was part Irish, was made), but there's a lot of confusion about what being "made" really meant. In the old days there would (so I had heard) be a big, formal ceremony, with religious overtones and blood oaths. But I would read later that by the late 1960s there was "no ceremony, no burning of the hand, forget about it. That may have happened in the old Mustache Pete days, in the 30's, but not anymore."[1] Even in 1975 bringing a non-Italian into the mob as "a friend of the Outfit" was pretty unusual, but in any event it was really a good feeling for me because it meant that I would be treated something like a made man, which told the Mafia world, "Don't mess with Little Joe College without getting permission from the Mob."[2] It was like I had some kind of official title, and I was really proud of it, though I wouldn't be broadcasting it to the world. I was obviously already an insider and treated with respect even without that credential, but saving Duff placed me in a special, protected position. Nobody could screw with me without getting reprisal from the Mob—quite a position for a young man to be in. My growing reputation had led to more and more important jobs, and now I was a friend of the Outfit. I finally had High Hopes. I went home to my family that night and took everyone out to dinner. What I couldn't know then was that my saving Duff would ironically set in motion the chain of events that would lead to the end of my Chicago days.

All through this period I occasionally returned to my hometown of Dingess. Spry went back more often than I did, because he still had business there. Duff would accompany me to Dingess three times, twice before Sam Giancana's death in June 1975 and once after. The first time I took the five-hundred-mile trip from the Heights to Dingess with Duff was during the spring of 1975. I had bought a car for my younger brother and had to figure a way to get it to him. After Bob moved into my rental house, we got to know each other as coworkers must, having a few drinks together now and then and a meal or two. He didn't have a family to take care of, so one Thursday while we were having a drink in the Vagabond I asked him, "Hey, Duff, I just bought a car for my brother and thought if you're doin' nothing this weekend, you might like to drive the car for my brother to West Virginia while I drive mine. We'd stay the weekend in the metropolis of Dingess," I said, "and see the sights, such as they are." I figured it was best to stay on Duff's good side.

"Naw, I'm not doin' nothin', and I'd be glad to drive the car for your brother. I could use a little time away from the Heights."

The next Saturday morning we met at my place. Bob got in my car and I got in my brother's car and we headed out to drive straight through to Dingess. We agreed we'd take turns driving the lead vehicle and the follow vehicle, and I have to admit I had a bitch of a time keeping up with Duff when he was lead. He had a heavy foot that was always pushed to the floorboard, and I was just waiting for the Indiana or West Virginia state police to nail our asses. About halfway to Dingess we stopped at a highway restaurant, and while we ate Bob told me a little more about his life growing up on Hungry Hill outside Chicago. I thought I had a messed-up childhood, but mine was a Sunday prayer meeting compared with Bob's. His father was seldom home, but when he was he beat the shit out of Duff two or three times a day and Duff wound up in the hospital several times. "Man, what a shitty life," I thought, as we paid for the food and headed out to the cars for the last leg.

We pulled into Dingess, where I led Bob to my brother's place and turned the car over to him. My kid brother was so happy to get his first car that even Bob had to laugh at his excitement. We shot the shit with my brother and some of my family who still lived in the cruddy, old, tar-paper house where I grew up. After an hour or two we said our goodbyes, gave hugs all around, and Bob and I piled into my car to drive the ten miles or so to a small motel on the outskirts of Dingess. After checking in we dumped our stuff off and hit a couple of the local clubs for some good country food and a couple of bottles of local beer. About two in the morning we called it a night, went back to the motel, and hit the hay.

The next morning we got together about nine thirty and grabbed a country breakfast at the local diner where my sister worked. She was off shift, but when I told a couple of people that I was her brother, they couldn't do enough for us. Bob and I stuffed ourselves on the down-home breakfast special of fried eggs, grits and gravy, orange juice, and coffee.

On the second night in Dingess we stopped at a little hole-in-the-wall club owned by Dick Spry. Dick called me over to the bar. "Hey, Dick. I got someone I want you to meet. This here's Bob Duff. He and I drove down here to deliver a car for my little brother, so you treat him good, hear?" The two shook hands and Dick ordered a drink. We chatted for about three hours, with me breaking off every twenty minutes or so to shoot a game of pool with a couple of local geezers who were too drunk to shoot worth a shit. Easy money. I had just finished a game when Dick waved me to the back, and we went out into the chilly West Virginia night.

"Your buddy, Duff, seems like a cool guy. Can I trust him?"

I said, "You can trust Duff with your life. He's a real stand-up guy." I wasn't about to give Duff any reason to think I didn't trust him, though I didn't.

"Are you sure?" he shot back, "'cause we got some serious business going down."

"What kind of shit?" I asked.

Dick answered, "Just shit," meaning none of my business.

"OK, you guys talk it out," I said and went back inside to the pool tables, where one of the geezers handed me a pool cue and said, "You're up, kid," and I broke the rack. I had to work to keep a straight face, because those old codgers were so pissed that they could hardly get the cue on the table for a decent shot. I offered up a small wager.

I looked up from the table after a shot and through the plate glass window I saw Dick and Bob out on the back porch in a long and intense conversation.

I went to the glass door so I could see them a little closer, and they were looking at that .22-long, the High Standard pistol, the one with the home-made silencer. Later that evening I handled it myself, turning it over in my hand. Both of them shot the gun repeatedly, in back of the club and out front along the dirt road where the bar stood. There were no police around to say otherwise. The silencer, probably crafted from a lawn mower muffler, made the gun distinctive. Dick had won the gun in a poker game with Vance, and Duff could see its utility right away and was used to taking what he wanted; whether he "bought" it from Spry and didn't pay him for it or cheated him out of it I don't know. Dick and Bob talked for the rest of the night, taking turns buying each other drinks. I came into the conversation every thirty minutes or so, spending the rest of the time at the pool table. It looked like Bob and Dick were getting along pretty well.

The evening wore on, and finally Bob and Dick exchanged phone numbers and addresses as I headed for my car. Carrying a brown paper bag, Duff caught up with me and got into the shotgun seat while I walked around the car and got in on the driver's side. As I pulled my door closed, Bob stuffed the brown paper bag under his seat. After I started the car I nodded toward the brown bag. "What's that?"

"It's a pound of pink pussy," he shot back. He lit up a cigarette and flipped on the radio, ending the conversation. Dick had followed us to my car, and Bob rolled down his window to yell at Dick, "Stay cool, you red-headed son of a bitch; we got a lot of work to do."

"Yeah, don't sweat it," Dick replied, "I know what the hell I'm doin'."

With that, I gave a screw-you wave to Dick, gunned the motor, shot out of the parking lot, and headed back to our hotel. We grabbed our gear, paid the tab, got back in the car, and headed to Chicago Heights. We had barely used the room; back in the day, we stayed up two or three days at a time and thought nothing of it. This was one of those trips.

On the way back to Chicago, Duff and I continued the conversation about our childhoods and people we worked for. He asked if I had ever done any "work." I was still a little green and talked about some work I had done, realizing midsentence he didn't mean just "work." He cracked a grin and laughed in a way that said I was a pussy because I had never killed anyone. Then he started talking about his early times with the Mob. With an air of indifference Bob said, "I made my first hit when I was thirteen and working for Frankie Laporte, Capone's old chauffeur and bodyguard." At sixteen Duff had already killed six people for Laporte and, by that tender age, had acquired a sinister reputation. He bragged about the Mob sending him out only for the bigger jobs and how nobody messed with him because they knew he would shoot them in a heartbeat.

❧ ❧ ❧

HE TURNED UP the radio, dialed in a station, and we listened to doo-wop music all the way down Route 30, Chicago Road. We got to the Heights around two in the morning and pulled into the parking lot of the Liberty. Gus, the owner, was over in the corner reading a newspaper, and when he saw us come through the door, he called over, "Hey Charley, hey Bob, what you guys been doing, chasing pussy all night?"

"Naw," said Bob, "we just got in from Hillbilly Heaven, West Virginia, where Charley grew up. What you got that's good, Gus?"

"If you wanted something good, you shouldn't have come to the Liberty," Gus said with a big toothy smile. "How about eggs, bacon, toast, and coffee?"

❧ ❧ ❧

IN THE MIDDLE of May 1975, Duff and I went back to West Virginia, this time at Duff's suggestion. He wanted to get together again with Spry at the bar. I began to notice how much private time Bob and Dick took away from me during that trip. They were up to something, but it wasn't my place to ask about it.

I spent the next morning in Dingess visiting some of my family, and about noon I picked up Bob at the motel and we headed back to the Heights. During the drive back Bob was a lot quieter than he had been on the earlier trip, and he seemed lost in thinking, planning something he was not going to tell me about.

After we got back to the Heights we both returned to our normal routines and ran into each other only at Vergie's or the Ventura Lounge. I didn't know it at the time, but Bob was getting ready for his biggest hit yet, now just a few weeks away. And he'd brought Spry into it.

12. I'M THE GUY

A few days after we returned I asked Bob to drop me off at the track and to pick me up after the fourth race at the exit to the parking lot. It was a beautiful evening, and I was excited. Racing always did that to me. So, after four races that came out exactly the way I wanted them to, I picked up some money, shook a few hands, and walked to the parking lot to meet Duff, who had parked the car at the gate. It was about nine thirty in the evening. I had won a lot of money, so it was good to know that Duff was around for some added protection.

He took one look at my face and said, "You musta had a good day."

"Yeah," I replied with a smile, "a very good day." We walked to the car and talked about horse racing. When we approached my car, Duff said, "Hey, Little Joe, lemme drive."

"Sure," I said, "help yourself."

As Duff slipped the car into gear and headed down the gravel road between the rows of cars, he looked over at me and said, "Hey, Little Joe, there's gonna be a meet. I don't know everyone who's going to be there, but I do know that Tocco, Nick, Barrett, and I will be there."

"Am I gonna be there?" I asked.

"Hell, I don't know," he said, as he pulled out onto Chicago Avenue and headed for the Vagabond Lounge.

Now, I'd been around long enough to know that a "meet" was not a simple get-together. A meet meant something big was going down or someone had stepped out of line and was going to get disciplined. As it turned out, Barrett did not attend the actual meeting—he was downstairs at the Vagabond with Al Tocco. Tocco was usually the coolest guy around, but this evening he looked uneasy. As we came into the lounge Bob said, "I think Tocco wants to see you. I'll see you later." He went upstairs, and I went over to where Joe Barrett and Tocco were standing. They were talking in earnest with another man, a big barrel of a guy I didn't recognize, with a gray fedora hat and a tight-fitting sport jacket. I waited out of earshot so they could finish their conversation in private. Finally, Joe and Tocco shook hands with the big guy, who gave me a scowling glance as he passed. "To hell with you," I thought.

As I approached my two bosses, Tocco said, "Hey, Little Joe, I'd like you to do us a favor. I want you to go over near the Rancho Grande nightclub, about ten minutes away from the Vagabond." Tocco looked me straight in the eye and was very specific in his instructions. "OK, Little Joe, here's what I need you to do. Go straight from here and pull up near the phone booth on the corner across from the Rancho Grande. Leave your motor running and flash your lights twice and a guy will come over to your car. Don't get out. Just sit there with the window rolled down. He will come up to the car and say, 'Are you the guy?' And when he does, I want you to say, 'Yeah, I'm the guy.' Then he'll ask you again, 'Are you the guy?' and you say, 'Yeah, I'm the guy.' *Use those exact words.* The guy who comes up to you will then get in the back seat of your car; you drive him straight to the rear of the Vagabond Lounge and pull up to the fire-escape door at the back of the lounge. Barrett will meet you there."

"And one thing more," Tocco said, "No guns, no friends, just yourself, and remember," he said, "you don't need to make a lot of talk along the way. When he asks you 'Are you the guy?' You tell him, 'Yeah, I'm the guy.' That's it. Those exact words. Get it?"

I already figured I was supposed to keep my mouth shut in the car because this visitor didn't sound like a guy with whom you made a lot of small talk. Tocco added, "We'd consider it a favor, Little Joe," and then added, "Are you sure you got it to the letter?"

"Yeah, I got it. *I'm the guy.*"

"And, one more thing, Little Joe," he said before I could turn away. "After you make that pickup, forget about it." He paused. With a half-smile he said, "Well, get going." I turned on my heel and headed toward my car.

I DROVE QUICKLY to the pickup spot, pulled over to the curve, left the engine running and pulled down the driver-side window. I flashed my lights twice. A brief thunderstorm had passed through the area earlier, and the streets were still wet and shining. A group of three or four revelers were leaving the Rancho Grande around Halsted and Sixteenth, obviously a little soused.

It was around 10 P.M. I sat there in the car looking straight ahead. Nothing happened for about three minutes, and then in the left rearview mirror I saw a shadow approaching the car. In my rearview I caught a quick glimpse of a middle-aged guy in a blue or black suit. He stayed a little back from the window, like a cop giving a ticket. "Are you the guy?" "Yeah, I'm the guy," I said, looking straight ahead through the windshield.

The rest of the pickup went exactly as Tocco had said. Twenty-five minutes later I was pulling into the back entrance of the Vagabond Lounge and sure enough there was Joe Barrett waiting outside for my passenger. I caught just a half glimpse as he got out on my side of the car. I remember thinking to myself, "This guy must be some kind of big wheel when Joe Barrett meets him at the back door." I waited in the car for the mystery man to get out and shake hands with Joe, who turned and led him into the lounge. I looked back through my rearview. The man looked straight back at me with a cold stare, so cold I had to turn my eyes away. He and Joe went into the Vagabond. Still, he sure didn't look like a "wiseguy." Too smooth, too handsome.

And that was all there was to that job. My silence was all that was needed.

Duff would later fill me in on the purpose of the meet and the identity of my strange passenger. He was none other than Johnny Roselli, "Handsome Johnny" or "the Snake,"[1] a close associate of Anthony Spilotro and a big player in the Mob's move into Las Vegas and then California.[2] The meet was to discuss bringing down Sam Giancana, the most storied gangster of his generation, and Roselli was there to see that it was done right. And Duff was there to receive his assignment: Kill Sam Giancana.

THE SUMMER OF 1975 was the last good one I would have for a long while. I was so busy I didn't notice the storm clouds gathering over the Outfit. I was never much of a reader, so as I went about my own life I was oblivious to the front-page comings, goings, and hospital stays of the "retired" boss of bosses of the Chicago Outfit, Sam Giancana. I heard a lot of street talk but had no context to understand how his overarching presence in the world of organized crime would intersect with my little part of it, nor could I predict the part I would play in his demise. As I read the newspapers my mind reached back to the first time I heard Giancana's name, on that golf course with Columbus when I was a kid. Columbus hadn't been there to play golf. A lot of Outfit guys liked to meet on the golf course because it was harder for law enforcement to listen in. Columbus took me everywhere with him in those days, but I thought it was because he loved me like a son, and I still believe that was part of it. But guys in his world were also known as good family men, with lots of kids and the semblance of a normal home life, and you were much less likely to get whacked if you were in the presence of family. In fact, it was a point of honor, and shocked even Outfit guys when a spouse (as with Billy Dauber's wife) or child is taken out along with the intended target.

Surely it can't have been Giancana himself who delivered the money to Columbus? But I have no doubt, looking back, that Columbus was telling me the real source of the money, sure that a kid had no one to tell, even if I had understood at the time. I still don't know who came to West Virginia with Giancana, and I have no written evidence Giancana was there personally, but the best supposition I've heard for who came with him and handled the cash was his associate Paul "Skinny" D'Amato, who was in charge of handing out the vote money on Sam's behalf in West Virginia.[3] Skinny was one of the people who came to Frank Sinatra's aid when he had trouble finding work, booking him into the 500 Club in Atlantic City.[4] Chicago money poured into West Virginia and bought more than enough votes to swing the 1960 Democratic presidential primary vote from Hubert Humphrey to Kennedy; I believe Columbus was in charge of distributing that bag full, $35,000. Columbus was connected both with the Chicago gang and with the looser element that gathered around Claude "Big Daddy" Ellis in Logan County.[5] I have little trouble believing Albert Tocco's tentacles reached deep into West Virginia and delivered the state to Kennedy, with Columbus's help.[6]

As I paid more attention in the years that followed I realized that when the name Giancana was spoken it was with a mix of fear and respect. Giancana led one of the most colorful lives in American history, and the paper trail of his life is immense. I will leave the reader who is interested to delve more deeply into it, but it can be summarized fairly briefly. He was born in Chicago to Sicilian immigrant parents. He joined the so-called Forty-Two Gang, a street crew of tough kids, in the 1930s and soon became a trusted getaway driver and a ruthless murderer. He and his gang gradually insinuated themselves in the Chicago Outfit.

He served time in prison in the early 1940s and on his release went right back to helping the Outfit take over lotteries and other rackets in Chicago. He was ambitious: his ties to Frank Sinatra and show business probably began soon after. Giancana often bragged about having several police chiefs under his thumb, in addition to what must have been hundreds of police officers. During the Kennedy administration Giancana developed an association with the CIA and was purportedly involved in the plot to assassinate Cuban president Fidel Castro.[7] Giancana is reported to have said that the CIA and the Mob are simply two sides of the same coin, and he may well have thought his assistance to the government would protect him and his business. And it did, for a while. In the numerous files that have become public in recent years, it's claimed that Giancana and JFK shared a mistress, Judith Campbell Exner. (She was also well acquainted with "Handsome" Johnny Roselli.)[8] She acted as a go-between for the president and the top echelon of organized crime. Giancana's relationship with Hollywood and Washington grew as Kennedy's political star rose. Giancana loved show business, and it was reported that Marilyn Monroe spent her last night alive with him,[9] his tentacles reaching coast to coast and into every avenue of American life, though few Americans knew it.

But he was deposed as Outfit leader in the late 1960s and spent seven years in exile in Mexico although still reportedly deep in all kinds of criminal enterprises before being arrested and deported back to Chicago. In 1965 Giancana had been jailed for refusing to testify before a grand jury despite saying he would do so and despite a grant of immunity.[10] On his release the Justice Department decided, over the objection of the U.S. attorney, not to pursue it further, a controversial decision the presiding judge called a "mistake" and "unwise."[11]

But Giancana's "trial" wasn't over. The *Chicago Tribune* reported that Mob leaders were to meet soon after to discuss deposing him: "In a sense, Giancana will defend himself against charges of having permitted his international playboy activities to interfere with the more serious, day-to-day business of running the underworld operation."[12]

Now almost ten years later, Giancana had already testified multiple times before a grand jury focusing on mob investments overseas, again under a grant of immunity, although a spokesman for the Justice Department said he "didn't say very much" in those appearances.[13] He would soon have been called to testify before a U.S. Senate intelligence committee looking into the connections between the CIA and the Cosa Nostra in plots to assassinate the president, among other things, and remains the only person killed just before he was to appear before such a committee. The committee chairman said Giancana had been "located" but not "interviewed" at the time of his death.[14] Whether he would have implicated other higher-ups in the Outfit or in government will never be known, as he never had the chance to testify to the committee.

On June 19, 1975, Giancana was in the kitchen of his house in Oak Park, Illinois, just outside Chicago. The police detail guarding his house was mysteriously withdrawn that night, and Giancana was murdered sometime around 10 P.M. It is speculated that the murderer was a friend of his, as Giancana wouldn't have let just anyone enter the house at that time.

He had lasted longer than many "retired" Mob bosses and was rumored to be back in business but not sharing any of the profits with the Outfit. His execution was, without doubt, the most notorious and publicized gang hit since the days of Al Capone, and one of the biggest unsolved crimes in American history. What was he about to spill? Or would he? Somebody wanted the question to go away, and we still don't know who did it, despite Giancana being under constant police surveillance. He was shot in the head and in the mouth repeatedly in his basement, peppers still cooking on the stove, when the caretaker, who had been upstairs all evening, found him lifeless. No sign of the murderer. He was buried in a silver casket that cost $8,000.[15]

The rise and fall of a mob boss, especially one connected and intimately involved with as many nationally known political celebrities and some of the world's most famous entertainment celebrities and power brokers as Giancana was, can never be explained with any finality. There are too many secrets surrounding it, too many people with a good reason to keep the truth hidden or make up stories so the real truth gets obscured. And for those reasons, and his association with Hollywood and politics, there has probably been more printers' ink thrown on paper about Sam Giancana, good and bad, right and wrong, than any underworld figure since Al Capone. In many ways his reign was more notorious than Capone's. And to think my little life would become entangled with his, over a little .22 pistol, was beyond anyone's imagination.

13. GOODBYE SAM, GOODBYE DICK

By late July of 1975 the deed was done; the papers reported Giancana's death in huge headlines, and every day that summer brought some new tidbit of information about it—and plenty of speculation. You'd think that, being on the inside of the Chicago Heights Outfit, I would have heard other guys in the Outfit talking about the Giancana hit, but that never happened. It didn't happen because if you were part of the Outfit you didn't talk about anyone else in the Outfit, or about anything that happened in organized crime. For most of us, the only time you talked about business was when you were receiving instructions from above or giving instructions to those below you. Sure, there was talk on the street, but not among the mid- and upper-level bosses, the ones who might actually know what they're talking about. None of us wanted to attract publicity in any way. Crime and criminal activities flourish best when they are unknown, unseen, and done in secret and in the dark. We also knew that crime reporters and their front-page stories about Mob activities attracted investigative reporters and then grand jury investigations, often followed by criminal prosecutions and long prison terms starting with the low-level guys and working their way up. A small leak of information to the street guys could cause trouble for the bosses later.

BUT GIANCANA'S DEATH was such a big deal we couldn't help but speculate on it. It's been conjectured that the mob was put out with Sam because of his visibility and media celebrity status. But also he was making multimillions with his offshore casinos and not sharing a nickel with the Mob. He just refused. I think it's obvious that along with his constant presence in the press, and his ego, Giancana was a pain in the Outfit's ass, which was not a healthy place to be. Since coming back from Mexico Giancana had become more and more arrogant and pious about his past achievements, hits, and casino success. In the mob world, Sam was beginning to be considered a dinosaur, as younger men came up in the ranks. There were some in the Outfit who wished to hell Sam had stayed in Mexico. And when he returned to Chicago he started making signs that he had intentions of taking over his old place as the top man in the Outfit. Personally, I have no doubt the order to take Giancana out came from Chicago, rather than Hollywood or D.C. or Vegas.

❧ ❧ ❧

THAT SUMMER OF 1975 I was plenty busy with my horses, my service station, and whatever work Nick or Joe or their associates needed done. I was always on call for those. So I was unprepared for a call from Duff late at night on June 19, the evening Giancana was killed. His voice was muffled like he didn't want to be overheard. He was whispering and sounded like he was hurt in some way. I knew something was wrong. I didn't know whether he was calling at the request of some higher-up, so I agreed to come get him. But where? I understood "Washington" something. Then Duff hung up. I waited for him to call back. A few minutes later he did, his voice still muffled. I kept asking him to speak up, but he kept whispering. I practically yelled at him, "Duff, get to a phone booth and call the Liberty. I'll make sure Nick and some of the guys are there."

I went to Nick and Mario and relayed the message that Duff was some-place trying to escape the cops, that he had called twice but was talking so low I couldn't figure out where he was or where I was to meet him. I said I had told Duff to wait twenty minutes and then call the Liberty, that someone from the Outfit would be there to answer the phone. I spent two hours driving around Washington Park with no sign of Duff, so I went home. Later I learned that Nick and Mario had come to pick him up near Washington Park and Washington Boulevard.

Meanwhile Dick Spry disappeared the same night. Just gone. This was curious in itself, because he would have told me if he was going back to Dingess. And when I saw him again, he wouldn't tell me any more about it. What a strange night that was. I could have asked Nick or Joe about it but thought better of it. It was probably something I didn't need or want to know. Little did I know how important the answer to those questions would become to me later.

-❧- -❧- -❧-

I NEXT SAW Bob about a week later. He showed up at the Vagabond with a swollen knee. He was really hobbling to get to the bar. I helped him to a barstool. "Thanks, Little Joe." I looked down at the injured leg and said, "Damn, Bob, what the hell happened to you?" He stretched the knee out with a wince and said, "It's a long story, Little Joe. Someday we'll talk and I'll tell you the story, but, until then. . . ." He warned me with that look of his that said, "That's all I'm gonna say."

Capisce. We had a few drinks, and before I took off for home Bob added, "Hey, Little Joe, let's go down to West Virginia. Let's go see Spry. I got something for him. You say when."

I was curious but agreed to go. I was clueless about his role in Giancana's death and busy with everything else in my life that July. Here I was, twenty-five years old, and my horses were doing great. The bosses were pleased with my racing action, and I followed their instructions closely. In addition, I had overseen several muscle missions that went without a hitch. I think the bosses were most impressed that I was able to get a target to cough up his street tax without my roughing him up. This Duff business was just a distraction, or so I thought.

-❧- -❧- -❧-

IN THE WEEKS that followed, the newspapers overflowed with stories about Giancana's murder. With no suspect in hand and plenty of people with motives, speculation was rampant about who had ordered it and who pulled the trigger. I read all the tabloids as eagerly as anyone else, of course, the details dribbling out: the execution-style message that came with a string of bullets to his mouth, a signal that he'd never live to rat on the Outfit; the peppers, still cooking, showing that the murder had taken place only moments earlier; Giancana's carefulness, even paranoia, indicating the killer was almost certainly someone he knew and would let in the house; the mysterious disappearance of the police detail watching his house.[1] Giancana clearly could have bought off half the Chicago police force. But the feds? The FBI? Clearly this was part of a game that took place well above my pay grade. I couldn't imagine Giancana's life touching mine.

It took me a while to notice, but it soon became clear that Duff and Spry were on the outs. Spry said Bob owed him money on the .22 pistol he had won from Roland Vance and passed on to Duff. There was a decided and bitter difference of opinion and a lot of bad blood between them. Bob said Spry had been paid everything that was coming to him, but Spry continued to bitch that Duff owed him for the .22. I could see why Duff had kept it—it was a perfect hit weapon. I didn't know what happened to it; Duff didn't have it with him that last trip to Dingess. I thought the whole thing very curious. It wasn't like it was hard for Duff to find a good weapon in Chicago. It seemed to come down to something very personal between him and Spry, but I couldn't figure it out.

I had tried several times to get Dick Spry to drive up to the Heights, meet with Duff, and come to some kind of agreement. Spry's response was, "You can tell Bob Duff to kiss my ass, because I ain't coming to the Heights and if Duff wants to see me, he can just drive to Dingess." I told this to Duff, who said, "No, I'm not gonna' kiss Spry's sorry ass by driving all the way to Dingess."

Al Tocco told me to come by. "We need to talk."

I couldn't turn Tocco down.

"Bob told me that this ass in Dingess is not a stand-up guy, and he says there's no way he owes Spry any more money for the gun. Bob says that Spry won't come here to the Heights, and if he wants to see Spry, he can go see him in Dingess. That's your hometown, isn't it Charley?"

"That's right, Al, and Spry tells me that Duff is being a horse's ass."

"OK, so, if Spry won't come here, will you take Bob to Dingess? 'Cause those guys have got to talk this disagreement out as soon as possible, 'cause me and Pilotto don't like bad blood in the Outfit." Al looked at me. "We'd consider it a favor." That phrase again.

Of course, I didn't hesitate. "Sure, I'll take Duff to Dingess."

You don't say no to Al Tocco.

THE FIRST TWO times I took Bob to Dingess he was an OK guy to be with; that would change when I took him to Dingess the final time, in the fall of 1975. By happenstance one evening I ran into Duff at the Vagabond and, following Tocco's prompt, told him I was going to Dingess the following Tuesday for my mom's birthday and asked him to come with me. Surprisingly, he said, "OK, I'll meet with Spry, but Spry had better stay cool." The expression on his face caused me no little concern, because when he said it his eyes narrowed in that menacing squint, which led me to ask, "You ain't gonna do anything stupid, are you Duff?"

"Naw, I'm not going to mess with Spry, 'cause me and him have had some cool times together and I've had some good times in Dingess."

I didn't see Duff that weekend because I spent most of my time at the track. I called him on Monday night and asked if he was still going and he said, "Yes, I'm looking forward to the trip, you can pick me up at the house. What time?"

"How about eight-thirty?" I asked.

"I ain't no farmer, Little Joe, how about nine-thirty?"

"OK, nine-thirty it is, but be ready," I shot back.

"OK, I'll be ready. See you tomorrow."

"See ya," and I hung up the phone.

The next morning, I got stuck in traffic coming out of the Heights and arrived late to my rental place where Duff was staying. I remembered that I hadn't been paid anything for giving Duff my house and made a mental note to slip a hint to Nick D'Andrea when I got back from Dingess. I couldn't know it then, but I wouldn't see Nick again for a long time.

I pulled into my driveway and gave the horn a short honk. After a moment my front door opened and an arm shot out with a forefinger in the air, meaning he'd be there in a minute. I doubted that, but it really wasn't long before Bob came out with a small bag and a medium-sized one. He pointed to the trunk; I popped the lid and then unlocked the side door. He got in and gave me what for most people would be a half-hearted smile, but for Bob Duff, who almost never smiled, it was a dazzler. He looked at me as he slid the seatbelt across his body and latched it. "You're late, asshole," he said.

I returned a half-smile. There was something metallic in the air like a thunderstorm was coming, but the sky was clear. I backed out of the driveway, threw it into gear, and sped down the street. "What the hell is up with you and Spry?" he demanded.

"Nothing big," I responded. "I just don't think you guys need to be pissed off at each other. We had some good times together." "Yeah," he replied, "We can cool it, but he's messed up if he thinks I owe him money. How well did you know him when you were kids, Charley?" I was glad to get past the issue of who owed who, so I began to tell him about my relationship with Dick Spry and his family.

After stopping to grab a couple of burgers we got back in the car and switched drivers, with Bob gunning the car out of the parking lot and up the on-ramp heading east. I winced a bit at the speed but chose not to say anything. He looked over at me with a half-sneer and said, "You remember those bastards who shoved me into the trunk of my car?"

"Shit, Bob, how could I forget that? It was me who pulled your ass out."

"Well, they ain't gonna mess with no one no more; I got all three of them, and I hit the leader's balls with a blowtorch before I put him away. I found them. But first I had to get a hold of Don Hammond, who may have been the one who put the hit out on me and sent those asses to ambush me. So me and Nick went to the Heights and paid a visit on that son of a bitch. At first, we roughed him up a bit, but he wasn't talking. So we taped his hands and feet, and I took a blowtorch to his balls. It wasn't ten seconds before he was screaming like a little girl, naming all three of those guys and how to find their hideout in Quincy. I figured we had all we wanted to know; so I left him there holding his burnt balls and crying like a baby."

"Holy shit, Bob," I said, "You torched his balls?" I was a little queasy.

"To a nice black toasty crisp."

"Jesus, Bob, remind me never to mess with you." I thought about it. Burned his balls, damn. He must have read my mind. "You saved my ass, Charley, I'm never going to mess you over. Two days later, I drove to Quincy and Don wasn't lying. They were right there where he said they would be. That was, of course, after we toasted his testicles," Duff said, with a sadistic little laugh.

"I found two of 'em together, scared shitless, when I walked into the bar where they were hanging out. I shot both, one in the head and the other one in the stomach so he could live for a while to tell me where the third one was. I reached down and pistol-whipped the guy I had shot in the stomach. 'Where's that third bastard?' and smacked him across the bridge of his nose with the muzzle of my gun. That did it. His nose started gushing blood; that loosened his memory, and he told me where his buddy was and, as soon as he did, I shot him in the head, too. I went to where he told me the third son of a bitch was and killed him, too. The bastards were not going to screw with Bob Duff. They weren't going to mess with anyone again."

Now, whether Duff shot Hammond after he got all the information he needed, or whether he took him to Quincy, I don't know. I assumed he killed him, because I never heard of Don after that. Of course, people came and went, and I too would soon be taking an extended leave of absence from the Heights. I chose not to press Duff.

Changing the subject, I asked, "How did you get started in the rackets, Duff?" He told me about his time in the Air Force and about robbing the payroll of an airbase. I assume he was telling the truth, because Duff was always matter-of-fact about his exploits. He also told me about going to prison more than once, and it seemed no big deal to him.

On the way to Dingess we got caught in a long traffic pileup on Route 10, and after we inched forward for almost an hour we finally got to the tie-up. It was a caused by two guys heisting a mail truck. They kidnapped the driver and left the truck in the middle of the road. The tie-up made the trip from the Heights to Dingess an hour or so longer, so we didn't get there until about seven thirty. By that time neither of us felt like going out, so we went to the Hotel Princess Aracoma and hit the hay.

The next morning we had something to eat and went to Dick's place, where I parked my car and the three of us rode in Spry's car to Logan, about twelve miles away. Spry was driving, and I was sitting shotgun, with Duff in the back seat behind Dick. We headed for the Mecca Drive In where my sister worked as head waitress. Duff and Spry acted as though they had something to say in private. Finally Spry said, "You wait here," and he and Duff went outside the restaurant to talk. They talked alone for about twenty minutes while I talked to my sister and some old school buddies. Every once in a while I glanced out at Spry and Duff, who looked like two banty roosters strutting around each other and making wild gestures.

They motioned for me, and we left the Mecca. As soon as I got in the car I could see that they both looked very mad and were quiet. You could have cut the tension in the air with a knife. I asked if everything was OK. Bob said that everything was fine and that they were just going over some things, so I just said, "OK.'"

We had driven about six miles when Dick pulled over and they both got out. They were going to bring their quarrel to a head. They walked and talked, circling and cussing each other for about thirty minutes under a darkening sky that was threatening a rain squall.

I knew there was a major problem and that I was supposed to settle it. I knew they both had guns. That wasn't good. When they got back in the car and we started up the mountain, Dick said to me, "Hey, Charley, don't bring this guy back to Dingess ever again."

"Spry, I'll go where I want to," and back and forth it went. Suddenly, Dick pulled over, stopped, and as soon as the car was in park, he told Bob to get out.

Bob didn't get out. Instead there were three flashes and three loud bangs. Pop, pop, pop. Before I knew what was happening Bob had pumped three shots into the back of Dick's head. The flash and noise blinded me, and I was deaf for a few seconds. I was sitting in the right front passenger seat, and the next thing I know Bob was holding a pistol to my head and telling me to push Dick's ass out and drive him back to my car.

My friend's blood was all over the front seat. Hunks of his brain were dripping down the windshield. I had seen a lot in my short life, but I was in shock. Bob wasn't playing, so I did what I was told. Reaching across the pile of gore, I grabbed the driver's side door handle and the car door swung open. By this time, Spry's body had slumped over the steering wheel and slid to the right and got wedged between the steering wheel and transmission hump that separated the leg wells of the two seats.

From this position, I could see the back of Spry's head still gushing blood and part of his greyish brain still pulsating. I pushed and heaved a couple of times, but his body refused to move.

Duff was still screaming, "Push him out into the street, and let's go. Now, asshole."

"I can't, Duff; he's wedged in. Let me get out and pull him out from the driver's side."

"OK, but I've got this pistol pointed at you all the way. Don't try nothin' funny."

"OK, OK," I yelled back. "Cool it."

Then he demanded, "Go around the front of the car, not the back."

I got out on the shotgun side and as Duff hit the electric window buttons, I saw the barrel of his snub-nose .38 follow me around the front of the car. I stopped only for a second to throw up. I yanked open the driver's door and reached in around the steering wheel, pulling the now-lifeless body of Dick Spry toward me. As I pulled his shoulders his head flopped back toward me and sprayed blood and brain all over me. I took off my jacket and tried to sweep and mop the blood and gore out of the seat, but Duff pushed the pistol into my face and yelled, "Get in and drive. Now."

The smell of blood was fouling the air, and I heaved my guts up once more before we got to Dick's club. Duff kept the .38 on me all the way to the parking lot. I got out of the car and told Duff I had to get some of the blood and brains off me, so I opened the trunk of my car and grabbed my travel bag. I walked to the edge of the parking lot where it dropped off into a small creek. It was cold, but I dunked myself in the creek and got rid of my bloody clothes in the nearby bushes. I grabbed some clothes from my duffel and got dressed as fast as I could, because Duff was already yelling for me to get back in the car.

Duff was leaning back on the right fender of the car with his gun dangling in his hand. As I approached him, he pointed the gun carelessly at me and said, "Sorry, Charley, but I couldn't take any more of his shit. Look, I got to get back to the Heights, and I've got to have some guarantee that you'll keep your mouth shut."

"Duff, you know I'm not a squealer."

"Yeah, I know, but I have to have some kind of guarantee. You got family here, right?"

Getting them involved was the last thing I needed, but I was desperate. "I'll tell you what, Bob: we'll go to my other sister's place and I'll get her to drive back to the Heights with you."

I knew he wouldn't hurt my sister, because he knew I would kill him if he did. I was trading her as a hostage for my own life. But as I say, I was desperate. I took some more clothes and found some rags to clean the car as best I could, which wasn't very good. We piled into the car and drove to my sister's, me driving and Duff riding shotgun. In about fifteen minutes we got to my sister's house and knocked on the door. She was surprised to see us and wasn't too keen on an unplanned trip to the Heights, but she went upstairs to pack a bag.

She didn't take long. Bob and my sister got in my car and he punched the driver's side window open and said, "Keep your mouth shut!"

He had that determined look on his face, as if he'd just as soon shoot me as have to worry about me talking. "Hey, Bob, you know I won't squeal; my lips are sealed. You've got my sister and my car, how am I gonna squeal? You know me, and you know I won't squeal, ever! Not ever! I'll stay here and keep my mouth shut."

I had the presence of mind to remind Bob that he owed me for pulling him out of that burning car. He gave me a long, hard look. "OK, keep your mouth shut," he said. He hit the gas and peeled out for the Heights, my sister in tow. I was back where I started, in Dingess with nothing but the clothes on my back and a dead friend just up the road, his blood and bits of brain and thin strands of red hair barely dry on me.

I was thinking as fast as I could, but was still in shock. Why stay in West Virginia? What was my next move? Did I have a next move?

The question became moot immediately. It was just a matter of hours before I was picked up by the state police, and Duff was arrested just days later in Illinois.[2] That's what I get for being a good guy, relatively speaking. This was too messy a job to be covered up. The police were hell-bent on getting a conviction. It wouldn't have mattered, not in that county, whether the person was actually guilty or innocent; someone had to go to jail. Maybe Duff would risk his own hide only to protect someone more important than me.

The police knew I wasn't the killer and that I wouldn't tell them who the shooter was. They charged me with first-degree murder and threw me in the slammer. I wanted the cavalry: Albert Tocco, the guy over Nick and his crew, had judges in his pocket all over the place, including Logan. But in my case he didn't pull the strings I hoped for.

With the clang of those steel bars, in an instant I lost my business, my family, my horses, and, I guessed, my life. Here I was, in a hick town where I had made enemies, the last place on Earth I wanted to be, framed on a murder charge by a state police who didn't give a shit if they had the right person as long as they had someone to hang it on.

After a few phone calls and, of course, the *Logan Banner* newspaper's reporting of the crime, I had few secrets left. I sat in solitary; no phone, no family, no friends.

One day an attorney named George Pertain came in to see me. "Charley, you shouldn't be here; they got the wrong man. In the morning, I will file a writ of habeas corpus." And sure enough, the judge set me free the next day. I was flying, I was so happy. It seemed that Tocco's long tentacle had once more reached down into the hills. But my good fortune was short-lived, because as soon as I hit the sidewalk I was picked up and charged with the same thing all over again. I don't suppose I have to say what was going through my mind. My life seemed over. Everything that I loved or cared about was gone, a wife and four kids torn from my life.

After another night in confinement, God sent me a guardian angel in the form of another attorney, J. Ned Grubb, the F. Lee Bailey of Logan County, the same Ned Grubb whose twin daughters drove their car into a stump next to the sawmill where I worked. No one can imagine the relief I felt when I saw his face, the relief of having an awful burden lifted. If anyone needed his help, I did. He knew that Cannonball Jeffries and I had held his daughters in our arms as they died. I think in the intervening years he should have looked us up and talked to us about their last moments, but he never did, perhaps because it was too painful. Maybe he always felt a little guilty about that. Almost ten years had passed when we met again in that courtroom in Logan, but when he saw me he instantly recognized me. His first comment to me was, "I'm your lawyer, and I'll do anything I can to set you free." I had no money, but that didn't seem to be a problem. It wasn't twenty minutes before I knew he was in my corner, and I couldn't have had a better lawyer had I been able to employ Clarence Darrow. After checking the briefs and the court documents, he said to me, "Charley, this is the most unjust case I've handled in my entire legal career. Sit tight; help is on the way. Whatever you need, tell this deputy. His name is Otto Mans."

Whether or not he had questions for me or information to give me, Otto came by my cell every day just to say hello, and I looked forward to his visits. One day he said, "If anyone in the state police try to question you, don't tell them anything. Nothing!" He didn't have to tell me that. We both knew one word from me would mean my death, inside jail or out.

After I'd spent many months in jail, Ned came to my cell and said, "Charley, here's the best deal I can get for you because the state police are bound and determined to put your ass in jail. They are pissed because they think you know more than you are telling, and they have been demanding a life sentence. They want life, and they have not budged and will not budge; so here's the best I can do for you. We have to accept the charge and plead guilty. If we do, they will accept a sentence of five years, but if you insist on a plea of not guilty, they will continue to ask for life, and you don't have much of a chance of beating their case." It turns out Duff had been indicted back in Illinois for the murder but refused to waive extradition,[3] and the bought-and-paid-for justice system of Chicago had nothing to gain by turning him over to some hillbillies in the middle of nowhere.

In the meantime, my wife hid my kids from me and the people I'd been associating with; under the circumstances I didn't blame her. I am sparing her the further burden of naming her or describing our relationship here.

"Now, Charley, on the good side," Ned continued, "I have friends in the statehouse. Once you get your sentence of five years with a guilty plea, after six months we will get you transferred to trustee status, and you will be released from prison and move into an apartment where you can live, provided you can keep your lips zipped about this. Forever." He looked me in the eye.

I said, "Christ, Ned, I am simply not guilty of anything. I'm pleading guilty to murder and getting five years in prison for trying to break up an argument."

Trying to placate me, Ned said, "Charley, listen to me; if we go to trial, they will use manufactured evidence to win over the attorney general. Take the five years and the case is closed. Forever."

I swallowed hard. I knew Ned was on my side and was right about my options, so reluctantly I took the sentence. Ned kept his deal, I kept mine, and later Ned became a judge and continued to do everything he could for me. I supposedly had no resources, but even while keeping the straightest of books for my service station and other legitimate businesses, I had tucked away a "savings account" in those Mason jars. I paid Ned for his services, and of course he wanted it up front; in return, he protected what was left of the cash I had buried until I got out.

But Ned couldn't work out the trustee status. I ended up spending five long, miserable years in prison and on work release. After my release in September 1980 I worked several jobs and began my journey to go straight. I put out tentative feelers, but my family in Chicago Heights had moved on, with a new address and new names. My old associates in the Outfit kept their distance. But I was determined to go straight, so I worked long and hard to make a clean start. I settled down in Beckley, West Virginia, a city of about twenty-five thousand people seventy miles from Dingess.

How many times did I turn it over in my mind during those years? There is not the slightest doubt that had I squealed on Duff, I would have been immediately killed by Duff or another member of the Outfit.

When I was released I was ordered to keep away from any criminal activities. But after I was off parole I went to retrieve, at great risk, a little over $100,000 I had amassed during my Chicago Heights days and had stashed in the National Bank of Logan with the help of my attorney while I was in prison. A week after my release I went hunting for a place to live and was finally able to rent half of a rather large Spanish-style house in Beckley owned by a man named Herrera. I had been away from any contact with the Outfit for more than five years. I was free, but despite the warnings by the court to stay away from any kind of crime I came to a conclusion: I had to confront Duff. I had to. My questions ate at me every day. No matter how hard I tried to get it out of my mind, my thoughts were constantly and continually full of a burning desire to find Duff and, one way or another, get him to tell me why he killed Spry and left me to rot in a West Virginia prison for the murder he committed. What the hell were they arguing about? What was so special about that .22? Duff and I had spent a lot of time together. He was responsible for my being in prison, and that bastard didn't even have the decency to write me a note or give me a call. To say I was angry would be an understatement. I had been on a slow boil, and now I wanted—I needed—answers. I tried and tried to get that obsession with Duff out of my mind, because I knew if I were caught associating with him my probation would be terminated and I'd be slapped right back into a West Virginia prison. I would also be taking the chance of being killed by one of the most malicious hit men I'd met in organized crime, one who had a secret he had to keep. I had seen his work firsthand, and I knew if he got pissed he would just as soon put five bullets in me as swat a fly. But, despite the risk, despite the potential consequences, after a time I became certain I had to find Duff and ask him, face-to-face, why he had killed Spry and abandoned me. The meek don't inherit anything but trouble, I thought. I had tried to act as peacemaker, and I saw where that got me.

The longer my obsession ate at me, the more certain I was that I would go back to Chicago Heights and find Duff. I figured he might be in prison someplace but wouldn't be for long; he never was. The trail had to start in the Heights. Duff was in prison, I'd heard, though my source was unreliable. As I thought about how I was going to get the answers I needed from Duff, I was comforted by visualizing him in prison, as I had been. Hell, he should have still been in prison for trying to kill Krask, much less all the other jobs he'd pulled.

But he wasn't.

14. WITH FRESH EYES

*I*ronically, going to prison may have saved my life.

I had left the Heights to languish in a West Virginia state facility for five years, "on vacation" as it were. For me it was a permanent vacation from the Heights, except for a visit I'll tell you about later. By the time I got out of prison in 1980, the world, and the Outfit, had changed. Racing profits had been cut by legalized off-track betting, and legal casinos trimmed illicit gambling revenues. The feds were pushing hard, and many of the Outfit's moneymakers were no longer so untouchable. The 1970 Racketeer Influenced and Corrupt Organizations Act, or RICO,[1] put away a lot of mobsters, and many chose the federal witness protection program, also created in 1970, over prison or being hit for informing.

There was competition from other gangs, too, and within Outfit crews themselves, all of whom were fighting over a diminishing pot of money. While I was "away at school" members of Al Tocco's organization were hit one after the other. Sam Guzzino, part owner of the Vagabond, for example, had his throat cut in 1981 when he was suspected of being an informant.[2] Only years later would many of the killings of the 1970s be considered resolved, as part the circus known as Operation Family Secrets.[3] The feds, who couldn't be bought off as easily as Chicago law enforcement and judges, were incessantly tailing high-level Outfit leaders. The 1980 hit on Billy Dauber, an assassin who was cooperating with law enforcement, brought even closer scrutiny.[4]

I had followed events in the Heights area from afar, and in the coming years the Internet would make it easier. I especially paid attention to new theories about Giancana, trying to piece it all together. All I found was speculation, however.[5]

I knew Chicago had changed since I'd been gone; things there were already changing when I left. Rival gangs multiplied and became more ruthless, though Outfit killers remained well protected by local politicians and judges.[6] Big money moved in from other cities and set up shop, running the rackets the local Outfit once owned. Every week in the Chicago papers you'd read about several guys riddled with bullets and flopped into a ditch to be found by the authorities or just rot where they fell. God knows how many bodies are just a few feet underneath the promenades and apartment buildings and shops that have grown up around my old haunts.

I planned a trip back to the Heights to look for the guys who had essentially raised me—Joe Barrett and Nick D'Andrea, especially. I would tell them I needed answers before I could get on with my life. I knew that I had a long trip ahead of me, because I had to go slow on the five-hundred-mile, eleven-hour drive from Beckley to the Heights, as I couldn't get even a speeding ticket, not with my record.

I knew I had to get permission from the Outfit's then-current bosses to meet with Duff, and I hoped they'd help me find him and set up the meeting. But since I had been in prison the previous five years, I did not have the foggiest idea of where to find the people from the Outfit I needed to see, not a clue. Some of my old hangouts were gone—the old Vagabond Lounge had closed, and an ugly and unwelcoming new bar took its place under the same name. But one doesn't get sentimental in the Outfit. Many of my old gang were dead in the increasing violence of the chop shop wars or other turf battles, and in any event how would they take it for me to come start asking questions? Outfit guys don't go straight, or if they try to they usually don't live long.

I guessed the Outfit would have continued to use the new Vagabond as their main hangout and center of operations; I'd start there.

But I couldn't go into the Heights unprotected. There are rules you live by and rules you ignore if you want to stay alive. Felon or not, I was on my own and needed some muscle, and I felt comforted by the .38 I had tucked under the seat, just in case.

15. OLD HAUNTS

I left Beckley early on a Wednesday, planning to drive straight through to Chicago. I edged my 1975 Cadillac Eldorado, which I bought soon after my release, onto 77 North and headed toward 64 West. As I turned the heater up and turned on the radio, I realized that I was beginning a chain of events that if successful would bring me face-to-face with that son of a bitch Duff. Thinking back on that realization, I remember just a little chill of fear, because I was also setting in motion events that could very easily get me killed.

I told only a few people I was going back. One asked me if I planned to kill Duff when I saw him. I said no. This was not a hit mission. I was honest when I said it. I only wanted to know why Duff had killed Spry and left me holding the bag. But if I'm being stone-cold honest, I have to say that as I headed for Chicago I thought I would be seeing Duff in jail, into which I could not carry a gun, so the question was moot. Besides, I didn't want to go back to jail myself. But in the back of my mind I was also thinking Duff had better have a good story or I'd figure some way to do him in.

As I continued north toward Chicago my mind went over the events since Uncle Columbus negotiated my extraction from the poverty of Dingess. My uncle got me started on a life of crime in the Chicago Heights underworld, and there is no doubt in my mind that if it hadn't been for Uncle Columbus I would never have gotten out of Dingess. I might have ended up like my father, bitter and poor and drunken. I don't blame Uncle Columbus for my short-lived career with the Outfit; I'm sure he looked at the squalor and poverty in Dingess and thought nothing could be worse than living my life out in those miserable circumstances. And in retrospect, he was absolutely right.

As I passed by the sign that said I was entering Indiana I went back to thinking about Duff, and I could feel my blood pressure rise. My neck and shoulders tightened, and my hands started to sweat on the steering wheel. The feeling got a bit worse when I thought back to sitting in the shotgun seat of Spry's black-on-black 1974 Pontiac Grand Prix. I remember it clearly: I had just been looking down the road, not expecting anything. I remembered Duff ordering Dick to pull off the road, the roar of three shots in the closed car almost bursting my eardrums, then feeling the blood as it spattered all over the windshield and me. I remembered turning my head to yell at Duff, and I will always carry with me the maniacal look on his face. It was a look that haunted my dreams five years later, and still does. I think I saw in his eyes something of the world I never really knew, both from the perspective of the innocent people he (and I) shook down and from the perspective of a cold-blooded killer, a role I never aspired to.

-❧ -❧ -❧

I BLINKED, WATCHED the interstate disappearing under my wheels. It's amazing how a part of your mind can continue the mechanical job of driving while part of it is in another world. Then my mind jumped to how I would find Duff, and where. I wondered what he would look like and how he would act when I saw him again. I pictured him in jail, because that's where I was sure he would be. I knew this guy like the back of my hand and thought he would remember what I had done for him, rescuing him from the trunk of that burning car six years before. But I also knew he had a short fuse and a violent temper; so I could not truly count on any sense of his owing me.

Heading west now and coming up over a rise, I saw a restaurant just north of Indianapolis. My stomach told me I hadn't eaten in a while, and I needed a stretch break anyway, so I pulled off the highway and guided the Caddy to an open slot near the door. I ordered a quick burger and, because I was bored out of my head, made small talk with the plump blond waitress who brought me a piece of apple crumb cake. She reminded me of my ex-wife, whom I had not seen since I left the Heights and was grabbed off the streets of Dingess by the West Virginia state police. I felt a twinge of betrayal as I remembered I had heard not one word from my ex nor any of my four children since I was put in the slammer. Not one postcard, no birthday card, nothing. I tried to remember what my wife looked like the last time I saw her. I have a good memory, but her face was blurring now, indistinct, receding. I tried to imagine how each of my kids would look five years older than the last time I saw them.

But I soon realized I was just playing games with myself. The feeling of abandonment took away any pleasure in thinking about the past, so I set my mind on something else. I'm sure it was partially so I wouldn't feel the pain I must have caused them.

By this time the sun was fast dropping over the horizon and more of the cars heading toward me had their lights on. I flipped mine on too and laid the leather seat back a little to ease my cramped muscles. After several more hours of staying close to the speed limit the lights of Chicago started showing as an eerie haze in the distance. As I reached the suburbs the traffic increased and I got frustrated with the pace of the other cars. Take it easy, I told myself; your Chicago friends can't fix anything for you now.

Finally I pulled into the center of Chicago Heights and looked for a motel near where I remembered the Vagabond had been. I didn't have to look long because there was a Holiday Inn just around the corner. I parked the Caddy just short of the motel portico, checked in, and threw my stuff on the bed. Looking at the clock on the bedside table I saw that it was only 8:30, so I had a while before my old friends would turn up at the lounge. I grabbed a quick shower, put on some jeans and a loose gray shirt and tan jacket, left the key at the desk, and asked the desk clerk about the Vagabond. I had heard it moved to a new location. "Yeah," he said, bored and barely looking at me, "it's right across the street from where the old one used to be. You can't miss it."

In three minutes I saw the bank (First State Bank, later the Chicago National Bank) in the same building as the Vagabond Lounge and found a place to park the big Caddy just down the street. As I approached the new door of the Vagabond I felt a strange mix of feelings. Excitement, certainly, because for so many years the Vagabond had been my second home, where I got assignments, turned in money, partied with the guys. And I had felt safe there. Second, I felt anticipation because I hadn't been to the original lounge in five years, never in its replacement, and I did not have the foggiest idea of what I'd find. And, finally, I had a sense of apprehension, because I knew I was one step closer to my encounter with Bob Duff—an encounter I knew could bring danger. "Well, here goes," I thought. I pushed open the heavy doors, fancier now than the old, with *Vagabond Lounge* stenciled on the glass.

A quick glance around the room told me the new layout was totally different from the old lounge, and I didn't like what they had done. It looked like every other lounge now, not the familiar, seedy room I knew so well. I scanned the faces seated at the bar, people clustered around tables and talking. From long practice, I knew better than to sit in an exposed seat at the bar. I found a small table across the room where I would have my back to a blank wall and could study the people around the room in their varying states of intoxication. I felt certain that I wouldn't be noticed on this

Thursday night. A couple of guys looked vaguely familiar, but there was no one there I could remotely call a friend or even a past associate.

A skinny waitress with black hair and too much makeup brought me a drink, and when I asked her about a couple of guys I had known in earlier years she told me, in a voice that could cut glass, "I don't know no one, and I wouldn't tell you if I did." People don't cuddle up easily in Chicago. You learn quickly that things go better if you keep your mouth shut. I watched the room from my dark corner of the dimly lit room. Avoiding the harsh waitress, I walked over to the bar to order my second drink. When I was able to wedge myself into a space near the end of the bar, the bartender walked over to me, polishing a glass with a white bar towel. I ordered a Scotch on the rocks, and when he came back with it I leaned in and explained that I used to hang out a lot in the old lounge four or five years ago but I'd been away at "college." He knew what I meant. The bartender then asked, "Did you graduate?" which meant, were you out clean. "Yeah, I graduated," I said. Irony again, I thought: Little Joe College graduating from college.

After a while the bartender became friendlier with me when he found out that I really did have a lot of old friends he knew. It seems he had started work in the lounge very soon after I'd left the Heights and gone to jail. I continued dropping names of the guys I was looking for, but with no success. Finally, a guy walked in that I did know, Richie Guzzino. He'd been Al Pilotto's bodyguard. The Guzzino brothers worked as Pilotto's trusted chauffeurs and looked after him for several years—and they were the ones who apparently made the hit on him.[1] These were bad guys, I knew. I approached Richie, but warily.

I ordered a third drink, and we continued the "who do ya know," and I told him I was looking for Joe Barrett and Nick D'Andrea, for whom I had worked in the early seventies. Not long after I mentioned Joe's name, Guzzino said, "He used to come here a lot, but he's been in the hospital for a while with some kind of a goddamn liver problem." A few seconds later, still sipping his drink, he pushed a thumb toward the door, where a guy, maybe in his midforties and wearing jeans and a brown leather jacket, had just come in. "Hey, there's Joey," he said. Joey was Joe's son. "You can ask him about his dad." Guzzino waved the guy over to the bar and said, "Joey, this guy is Charley Hager. They called him 'Little Joe College' when he worked for your dad."

Joey and I shook hands, and he acknowledged that he had heard his dad talk about me a few years back. Then he brought me up to date on the major happenings with his father since I left and how his father's liver problems had gotten worse and worse until now he was in St. James Hospital. "Shit, that sucks," I sympathized with Joey. I told him I really needed to see his dad and asked if he could give his dad a call. Joey said, "Sure," and got the bartender to let him use the bar phone. While I waited for Joey to call his dad, Richie and I talked about trotting horses, but I could hear snippets of Joey's conversation with Joe in the background and it sounded positive. After a short talk, Joey put the phone down and came back to where Guzzino and I were sitting. "Hey, Charley, Dad said to tell little Joe College to get his ass over to St. James Hospital room 227 around ten tomorrow and you guys can shoot the shit."

Joey had a friend waiting at a table for him, so we shook hands again and said goodbye. I ordered one last drink, finished talking to the bartender, and poked a twenty into his tip glass. I went back to the table where I sat earlier and left a ten. One thing you learned in the Outfit: you never stiffed someone who did anything for you. All of the Outfit guys were big tippers. I waved to Joey, who raised a hand back, and headed out the door. I looked at my watch, saw that it was about eleven o'clock, and fired up the Cadillac to head back to the motel. I guess the adrenaline had kept the yawns away while I was in the bar, but a seventeen-hour day was starting to get to me, and I was ready to pack it in. Back at the Holiday Inn a bored night clerk gave me my key. I took the two-floor elevator ride to my room and called it a night.

The next morning I slept late and went to the lobby for the motel's continental breakfast. I went back to my room to hit the head, came back down, and got in my car. The St. James Hospital is only about half a mile from the Holiday Inn, and I got there a little before ten. I walked into the hospital lobby, located the hospital volunteers with their blue smocks and white hair, and asked them how to get to room 227. I found the right door and quietly knocked.

A voice I recognized immediately as Joe's answered with a quick, "Hey, come on in, Little Joe College." I pushed open the heavy hospital door, and there was Joe sitting on the side of the bed, looking pale but in good spirits. He was getting off the bed, and when he stood up he flashed me an enormous grin, threw open his hefty arms and said, "Hey, welcome home, Charley." It was clear Joe Barrett was happy to see an old pal, and after a hug and a kiss on both cheeks, I knew I was OK. Joe was happy, very relaxed, and asked, "What's up with you, Little Joe? How was the graduation party?," meaning last night at the Vagabond. I said, "It was great; they showed me a lot of respect."

"How's it going? Whatcha' been doing?" He pointed to a chair, "Sit down. Let's catch up."

I asked him how things were going with the lounge.

"Shit, it's awful, Charley. Everything has changed; it's a jungle out there. The Outfit's gettin' screwed all the time by the fuckin' blacks and spics takin' over everything and screwing up all the old neighborhoods with drugs."

Once we had caught up a bit he asked me: "Shit! Have you seen Bob?"

Have I seen Bob? That floored me. I said, "Hell, no, Joe, I haven't. I haven't been west of the West Virginia border for five years, but like Joey must have told you last night on the phone, that's who I'm here to see."

"Well," said Joe, rubbing his eyes with one hand and looking away. "That poor bastard. The big C's got him by the balls and he's pukin' his guts out and shootin' up every day. He's close to dead; he's real bad. Poor bastard looks like death warmed over. He lives over in a piss-ass shack in Richton Park, but he's in such awful shape, he'll have to go into a hospital or hospice pretty soon. His shit is done."

He looked back at me. "You look good, Charley."

"I feel good, Joe. Maybe college was good for me. But like I said I actually came here to see Duff. That's my only reason for coming back."

"Shit, I was hoping you wanted to come back and work with us again, Charley," said Joe with only a half-smile.

"Thanks, Joe, but after I see Duff I'm staying in West Virginia for a while." Joe looked serious and maybe a little distressed. He squinted. "It's about that shit down south, isn't it?" He knew full well that I was there to see him about Duff, and Duff about the murder of Dick Spry.

"Partly," I said, "but there's more, and I've got to get some answers and he's the only son of a bitch who can give them to me, so I'm asking your permission to go see him."

He didn't say anything. "Is there some problem with me goin' to see Duff?"

"Charley, you've always been straight with us. You're a friend. You can see Duff, and we'll help set it up. So give me a second." Joe picked up the hospital phone, dialed a number from memory, and was obviously talking to Nick D'Andrea. He gave Nick instructions about the meet, telling Nick, "Charley needs to see Duff, and I want no goddamn monkey business. See to that." He ended the conversation with an abrupt "OK, thanks."

About twenty minutes later Nick called back. Joe just listened and then said, "OK, thanks."

Turning to me, he said, "Nick has set it up with Duff for this afternoon. You need to go to Nick's place and see him for the details. Nick told Bob that you have our blessing, so there should be no funny business, but you know Bob. He's explosive."

"Yeah," I said, "I know that."

"Nick's got all the details, and he'll meet with you at his house."

We chatted a little while longer, but Joe knew I was eager to get on my way to Nick's and to meet with Bob. I thanked Joe. "You're a friend of ours, Charley. Anything for a friend." As I went to leave, Joe stood up and we had a man-hug and he said, "Watch your ass; it's a jungle out there."

A few minutes later I pulled out of the parking lot and headed for Nick's house. When I knocked on Nick's door I got a big welcome from Nick and his brother, who brought me a big glass of wine. We talked about old times for about an hour. Nick reminded me that Bob's house in Richton Park was the first house on the corner. I told him to give me a phone number just in case I got lost. Me, who had driven every neighborhood in town; but a lot had happened in the previous five years. Handing me a slip of paper, Nick laughed. "When you finish shittin' around with Duff, come see me; there's always some work around here for you." I didn't say anything. I still wasn't sure how far my old credit with the gang would last if they knew I was trying to get out of that life. And I didn't want to lie to Nick, who had been so good to me. Nick said, "I don't expect you to have any problems with that junkie. But do you want me to go along?"

"No, thanks," I replied, "I'm a big boy now, and I have a toy," gesturing slightly to the .38 under my shirt. Nick knew that I had my mind on one thing and one thing only, and that was the meet with Bob Duff.

"Watch yourself, Charley," Nick said; "things have changed out there."

"Yeah," I said, "it's a jungle and it's a lot thicker whenever that whacked-out Duff's around. Nick, did you say Duff's doing drugs? I never saw him do that shit."

"Yeah, he's on smack big time," said Nick. "I guess he's in big-time pain from the cancer, so I don't blame him none."

I stood up to go, eager to get to Duff. Nick gave me a big clap on the back as I went out his front door.

16. A BAG OF BONES CAN TALK

*I*t's hard to find words to describe how I felt to finally get face-to-face with the guy who had cost me my family and screwed up my life. Every thought, every bad intention that could ever surface in me came from every part of my body. I had a hundred questions: Do I get compensated somehow? Do I torture the bastard? Beat the shit out of him?

As my mind focused on what Bob had done to me, I got angrier and angrier. But I knew nothing good could come from these thoughts. I knew I couldn't let him read me, for he had been a master at reading people, with the animal instincts of a sociopath.

Duff's place in Richton Park was only about ten minutes from Nick's house in Chicago Heights, and I could feel the tension building up in me when I saw his house ahead. But my mama didn't raise no fools, and I drove past Bob's house looking it over as carefully as I could. I pulled into the parking lot of a supermarket telephone booth, next to the corner entrance.

I turned off the Caddy's radio, pulled out the paper with Bob's number on it, stepped into the booth, and dialed his number.

"Hello," a weak raspy voice answered. "Who's this?"

"It's me, Bob, Little Joe."

"Nick said you were coming to my place, Charley," he said, after a second or two of hesitation.

"Yeah, I know, but I'm in a black Cadillac Eldorado, near the entrance of the Smart Mart across the street. You gotta meet me here on neutral territory."

"I'm not feeling good," Charley, "I got cancer and it's killing me, so I don't go out."

"Yeah, I know, Bob, but you can get in the damn car and drive across the street! I need to meet you *here*. You understand that?"

"OK, OK," he responded, after another long pause. "Give me a few minutes to get my shit together, 'cause Cookie made me lunch and I'll be over."

111

"What you driving, Bob?" I asked.

"A yellow Cadillac Coupe Deville with a white vinyl top," he responded weakly.

"OK, Duff, I'll see you in about five minutes."

I went back to my car, turned it around so I could see the approach from Bob's house into the parking lot, and checked my watch.

After what seemed like an hour but was really about ten minutes, I saw the Coupe Deville coming down the street very slowly and then turn into the parking lot. The car pulled up a couple of yards from my rear, and as I was getting out of my car I heard the windows of Bob's car roll down. I reached down and slipped the safety off my .38.

"Stay the hell there," I called out, as I was climbing out of the Cadillac, "I'll come to you."

I walked around the front of my car, then around the back of Bob's car. I approached the open front window the way cops are trained to check you out during a traffic stop.

As I carefully peered down through the open window, watching for any sudden move Bob might make, I saw that he was not poised for anything. He was half slumped over the steering wheel, looking back and up at me over his shoulder.

When I got to his door I was just about to give him his instructions, but he spoke first. "Hey."

I said, "Hey."

He told me, "I've got to get back. Cookie's got a meal for me."

"Yeah, OK. You don't look good," I said, some real sympathy creeping into my voice.

"Shit! You wouldn't look good either if you had cancer every place in your body just waiting to kill you."

"That sucks, Bob. But here's the deal," I said, "I'll follow you back to your place. Stop in the driveway, get out, and wait for me to walk with you into the house."

Still hanging his head, he said nothing but nodded weakly and started his engine. I went back to my car and waited for him to turn his car around to exit the parking lot, and then I picked up his tail about twenty yards back. At the end of the parking lot he waited for traffic to open enough for both of us to get across the street. He then drove slowly toward the corner where he lived.

He turned right into his street and made another quick right into his driveway. I could see how hard it was for him to force the steering wheel into a turn and straighten it out again.

About five yards from his tiny back porch he braked to a stop, turned off the engine, and waited a minute or so until he could gather the strength to push down on the door handle and force it open. I reached down and instinctively hit the kill switch underneath the dash of my car to prevent anyone from starting the engine even with a key, all the while watching Bob's yellow Cadillac in front of me. After another long pause, Bob swung one leg out of the car, waited a few seconds, and followed it with the other. Fumbling around for his cane, he pulled himself up using the door as a support. With a huge effort he shuffled around the open door and walked slowly and painfully toward the house.

I caught up with him and, seeing how slowly he moved, relaxed a little. I saw how gaunt and emaciated he was and how hard it would be for him to make any sudden move. Still, I thought, the son of a bitch could be playing possum, and I warned myself not to let my guard down. I tried to see if he had a gun, but his loose-fitting jacket made that impossible. I walked a little behind him with my hand on his arm not less to steady him than to make sure he could not whirl around and shoot me. He may have looked like a dying man, but I couldn't think of him that way yet. It was hard to believe this was all that was left of the ominous figure, the seasoned killer feared by almost everyone, a man who had killed over a dozen people, three that I knew personally.

Bob's house was small, in a run-down area, and I was surprised that a big-deal Chicago hit man had fallen that far down the ladder. He maneuvered the three steps to the porch with obvious difficulty, paused for a second to get his breath and his balance, turned the handle, and pushed open the door. I walked in just behind Bob and held his arm as he staggered toward a chair behind the white kitchen table to the left of the door. He steadied himself again with a hand on the table, got to the chair, turned around, and flopped into it. The meal that his long-time girlfriend had fixed for him was still sitting at his place at the table—soup, rolls, and a glass of some drink I couldn't recognize.

I took a quick look around, with one eye on Duff. The kitchen was very small. The walls, floor, and ceiling were white, and, as I looked down the hallway, what I could see of the rest of the house appeared to be mostly white also. Typical of Duff, the kitchen was spotless. But, that was Bob Duff, a walking contradiction. He had been in the Army for several years in his younger life and neatness and order had been drilled into him along with, I guess, the capability to shoot to kill.

There were some pictures set around on the table and on the wall, including some of me and Nick and the others. I made a mental note that I'd like to have some of those.

He told me to sit down, pointing to the chair across from him, but I told him that I just had to stand after my long drive to Chicago from Dingess. The truth was that I wanted to have my back against the wall because I didn't know whether there was anyone else in the house and I wasn't taking any chances. With the kitchen light on him I got a better look. He was death barely walking. There was no spark, no animation whatsoever. He was wearing some kind of a faded flowery shirt which was not tucked into his plain brown pants, so I could not tell if he was packing. He spooned some soup into his mouth, but as soon as he did he choked, spit it out, and pushed the plate back.

I knew that getting this story would be a long, painful process for both of us, but I had no inkling of the surprises in store.

Looking up, Bob said his first words since we left the store parking lot: "Well, you did the time, Charley, and I owe you."

I was stunned. I had waited for those words for years, but now they seemed empty. As he talked, he went in and out of focus. He looked down at his plate, grabbed a small hunk of roll, stuffed it in his mouth, and in the same raspy whisper, said, "OK, Charley, you went through a lot of trouble with the bosses to force a meet. What's on your mind?"

What's on my mind? I thought. *You son of a bitch, you blew the back of my friend's head off right in front of me and landed me in prison for five years, and you wonder what's on my mind?* With that, the rage rose up in me again. I almost leaped at him to tear that frail body limb from limb. But I got myself under control. "I'm just here for some answers. For five years, I've been waiting for answers, and I don't want any crap. I want the truth. Why did you hit Dick, when you knew I'd brought you to Dingess to cool things down with him? And why did you let me rot in a West Virginia prison for a hit I didn't do and did not even know was going to happen. Damn, Bob, you stuck it to me, and you ask, 'What do you want?' That's crap—crap!"

"Yeah, I owe you," he repeated. "Charley, I want you to have my lock picks. I gave 'em to Nick. You can have them."

His lock picks? I didn't need them anymore. I wouldn't be returning to a life of crime. And they held no sentimental value for me.

"You owe me big time. But it's answers I want. Bottom line," I said, "Why did you whack Spry? This will be your repayment to me—case closed. Now tell me, goddammit."

Bob looked up at me with a strange expression. His body appeared to be fighting his mind, each growing weaker. This wasn't the man I knew five years ago. I still had small vestiges of sympathy for even the worst people I'd come across—one reason I'd never be an effective hit man. It seemed Duff could die any minute. What else can you do to a man like that? I must be the dumbest man on earth to even be talking to this half-dead piece of shit. But the truth was that whether he was sick or not, stoned or not, dying or not, I wanted some answers.

Duff sat stock-still, looking into the distance. I bent over closer to him as if to whisper but instead I yelled, "Wake up, asshole. Tell me about Spry!"

His eyes opened wider and focused on my face, "OK, Charley, I may not live to see tomorrow, but I owe you this. You did the time for the murder rap; here's the truth." He coughed and sat back. He sighed and took a moment to collect his thoughts. "Spry cut out on me."

"When? Where?" I snapped.

"OK, Charley," Duff responded, "This goes to your grave and stays in this kitchen. Spry ran out on me when we made the hit on Sam Giancana."

My jaw locked at the name, and for a moment I thought I'd heard him wrong. The hit on Sam Giancana? Damn, I thought, holy shit, could this puny guy in front of me have made the most famous Mob hit in years?

"You? You killed Giancana?" Was he just rambling, was he already out of his mind with the pain? Was he confusing Giancana with one of the many other hits on his résumé? I thought I'd humor him for the moment. "Tell me about it, you bastard."

"OK, but it's complicated and you gotta swear to take it to the grave with you, Charley. I have family, and I wouldn't want to bring any heat down on them." I responded with a vague promise, and he seemed to accept that.

"OK, here's how it went down." He was interrupted by a wave of pain. He clutched his stomach and held up a hand, asking me to wait. "I gotta have something for the pain. I need it now. Ya gotta give me a minute."

I'd waited this long; what the hell what was a few minutes? Besides, maybe the painkiller would make it easier for him to talk. There was no doubt he was desperate, and before I could answer him, he reached across the table and dragged a small cardboard box to him, turned it over clumsily, and spread the contents on the table. He pulled out a small silver teaspoon and set it in front of him, then a short candle and small butane lighter. With a shaky hand, he lit the candle with some trouble. He squirted a syringe of water into the bowl of the spoon, added a couple of chunks of brown stuff, and put it to one side. Then he pulled a brown leather strap from the box, wrapped it around his arm, and pulled it tight. He heated up the spoon and with the other hand reached down into the box, picked out another syringe, and drew the brownish liquid into its barrel. Then he stuck the needle into his forearm just inside the elbow.

He winced from the needle prick and then half-smiled a few seconds later as the heroin hit his bloodstream. He gathered himself, some of the old Duff showing through, and started talking.

17. WHEN YOU GOT A JOB TO DO, BETTER DO IT WELL

*D*uff told his tale, interrupted only by coughing spells and drinks of water. The story flowed out of him, almost like he was grateful to finally tell it.

He had waited his whole life for this one big hit. He said he got his marching orders directly from Al Tocco. Tocco told him he wanted no connection between the hit on Giancana and the Outfit. None. Duff didn't mention it, but I put two and two together, remembering my handsome, startling passenger. Johnny Roselli rode with me that night at the Rancho Grande. He was the messenger bringing the hit order to Duff.

Duff said he started by walking around Giancana's neighborhood in Oak Park in May, but as June approached his attention focused on the Giancana house, 1147 South Wenonah Avenue. At one entrance the house had a prominent doormat saying "Go Away."[1] About the tenth of June Duff noticed that the house just behind Giancana's was empty most of the day and evening. The unattended house was perfect to watch Giancana's because it was only about twenty yards away and at a slightly higher level. Duff could see what was happening on an hourly basis. Duff went back to his old lock-picking talents and used the borrowed house to put a tight surveillance on Giancana.

It didn't take Duff long to notice that both the Chicago police and the FBI were watching Giancana continuously. Although Sam was in Houston during most of Duff's vigil, Duff could get an idea of the comings and goings of Sam's cook, his driver, his gardener, and the caretaker who lived with his wife in an attic apartment. Duff was also able to get a feel for not only Giancana's staff but also the shifts of the police and FBI agents. Still, that wasn't close enough for Duff's liking. Late one day, he said, he went to a basement door at the side of Sam's house and found it unlocked and standing slightly open. (The existence of a "trap door" to Giancana's house appears to be true, according to a photograph in the *Chicago Sun-Times* and AP wire photos.[2]) The back door itself was apparently left ajar during the day sometimes to get cross-ventilation through the house; perhaps the staff may have forgotten to close and lock it, so Duff walked right in. This isn't as far-fetched as it may sound now, in hindsight, as I read later, "The Oak Park chief of detectives, Harold Fitzsimmons, said that it would have been easy for someone to enter the basement from an outside stairway without the caretaker hearing the noise above the air-conditioner and television. . . . Mr. Fitzsimmons said that Mr. Giancana had not been under police surveillance, although Oak Park police did drive by his home occasionally 'to see who was parked there.'"[3] Also, because it was a suburb, the Chicago city police had no jurisdiction, leaving the eventual investigation to the Oak Park police, Cook County sheriffs, and the state attorney.[4] Duff looked around the basement and ground floor, filing away in his mind the location of everything. He also stumbled on an extra set of keys and pocketed them.

As he continued to watch the Giancana house and neighborhood, as well as the rotation of police and the FBI visitors, Duff said, he knew he would have only one chance to pull this off and he had no intention of messing it up. Bob was disciplined in his vigil and careful not to leave any evidence of his having been in the house.

Meanwhile, Giancana seemed in a hurry for his meeting with destiny. Against doctor's orders Sam had sneaked out of the Methodist Hospital in Houston, Texas, where he was being treated for an abdominal aneurysm. He flew home to Chicago, where his two daughters and his driver met him at the airport. He set up house again on South Wenonah Avenue in Oak Park; his welcome-home party that evening would also be a farewell to this world.

Spry came back from West Virginia in a stolen or "borrowed" car he would use as the getaway vehicle and picked up Duff at my rental house. They drove to Oak Park the evening of June 19. They got there sometime between 9 and 10 P.M., circled the Giancana house, and went to the Seventh Day Adventist church at 1154 Wisconsin Avenue, just around the corner from Giancana's house. They parked the car and walked back to the house on foot.

In telling me the sequence of events, Duff didn't mention how the FBI and police detail were pulled away; it may be, as with most Outfit work, the fewer details he knew the better. It's impossible to think it was just luck the police chose those few moments to suspend their vigil. He probably would have told me if he knew who put a hold on the police for the hit. I believe Duff chose the time of the hit based on his observation of the house, the coming and going.

According to Duff, when he and Spry got to the Giancana house they simply went up to the front door and Dick hit the bell; almost immediately the door opened and there he was, Giancana, big as life but not for long, and staring at them in the dark. Maybe he was expecting someone else. "My heart leaped," Duff told me, "but we were sticking to the plan. We backed Giancana into the house and down the hallway. All Giancana could do was blurt out, 'What the hell?'" Duff pushed him back and held him against the wall and patted Sam down. He didn't put up much of a fight, probably because he was still weak from his operation and hospital stays.

Duff and Spry pushed Giancana down the stairs into the basement, with Duff's gun to the back of his head. The .22 with the silencer, the very one I'd handled back in West Virginia, the one that came from Vance to Spry to Duff. The very one Duff and Spry would argue over. The very one that got Spry killed.

All the time, Giancana was pleading, "You got the wrong guy! You've got the wrong guy!" I think he couldn't imagine who would have the balls to get to him like this. When they got to the basement Dick shoved Sam into a chair and kept his gun on him. The basement had a small kitchen. Duff told Giancana to shut up. He didn't.

Giancana started bargaining for his life: "I've got a lot of dough; it ain't here, but I can get it," according to Duff. "Sam tried to buy us off. 'More money than you ever dreamed of. Let me make a call. One call. I can have a pile of dough here in half an hour. Don't kill me! I'm worth more to you alive. Don't kill me. You've got the wrong guy! Who put out the hit? Let me talk to him. He's got the wrong guy.'"

In Duff's account Sam went to the stove, turned the fire on under peppers and sausages he had been cooking and started talking faster and faster to Dick and me about being hungry. "He was offering some to us, just trying to buy time to save his life."

Bob said he was totally unmoved by Sam's plea and just sat quietly at the kitchen table, all while Sam was cooking and offering Bob everything in the world, just so he wouldn't kill him. Duff remembered, "Two times, while we were talking to Sam, I heard one of the guys who worked in the house call down and say, 'Hey Sam! You alright down there?' Both times, I raised my gun in line with Sam's face and he answered, 'Yeah! Yeah! I'm OK, go back to what you were doing.'"

Duff said he and Spry let Giancana go on cooking, like cats playing with a mouse. I had the distinct impression Duff savored that moment, face to face with an immortal of the underworld—an immortal who was about to die.

Giancana, flamboyant in the company he kept but careful in his Outfit work, made his last mistake by turning toward Duff a little too quickly. Maybe Duff thought the hot skillet was the only weapon Sam could reach. "He just moved a little too fast," Duff said. "I wasn't sure he wasn't coming after me, but it didn't make no difference. It was time to put the bastard out of his misery and shut him up." Duff said, "Before he could fully turn, I shot him in the head. Sam dropped like a stone, but the guy seemed to have nine lives and I didn't trust him to be dead. I jumped over to him as he fell, flipped him over, jammed the .22 into his mouth and pumped more rounds into his skull, blowing the back of his head off. You can bet I knew the son of a bitch was dead then. Only thing is, I wrenched my knee like a bastard when I flipped him over. Hurt like hell." I was chilled at how matter-of-fact Duff was, like he was describing an enjoyable round of golf or a baseball game. A guy was bleeding out in front of him, his brains spreading across the floor, and he was worried about his knee. Both he and Spry would have Giancana's blood sprayed on them. I could see where he had gotten his cold reputation.

"I was so pumped up that the knee didn't really bother me until after the hit was done. I started looking around the house to see what interesting stuff I could find," Duff said.

"Jeez, why didn't you ice him immediately? You knew that's what you were going to do eventually. Why not just kill him? And why hang around?"

"That sounds right, Little Joe, but I thought the son of a bitch had money in the house. Maybe he would cough it up to save his life. A little bonus for me. But, shit, I guess he didn't. I think he was scared enough to give it up. And, after I took him out, I couldn't find any money and I guess I got mad and tore the place up." To the extent Duff was capable of looking sheepish, he did then.

And I can imagine what was going through poor Dick Spry's head at that point. He surely wanted to get out of there now that the job was done and was wondering how he'd come to hitch his wagon to such a mercurial guy as Duff.

"After we killed him I told Spry to go get the car and wait in the parking lot for me, and that I would be out in about 20 minutes. Go to either of the meeting spots and if you think there's trouble, cut out and go straight home." With that, Spry had gone back to the car. According to Duff he spent a

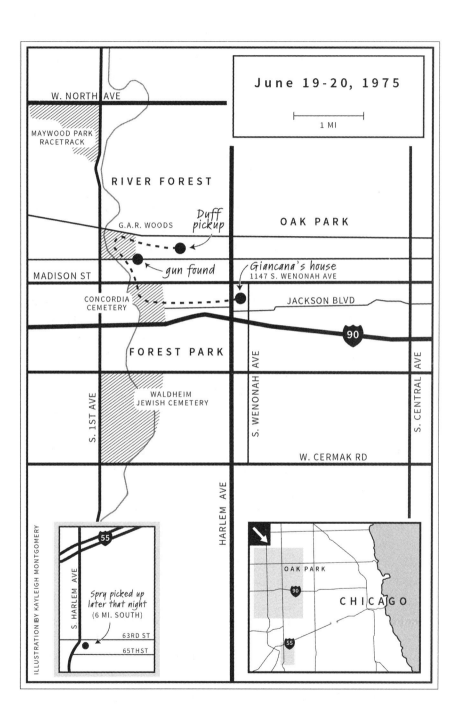

June 19-20, 1975

1 MI

W. NORTH AVE

MAYWOOD PARK RACETRACK

RIVER FOREST

G.A.R. WOODS

OAK PARK

Duff pickup

gun found

Giancana's house
1147 S. WENONAH AVE

MADISON ST

CONCORDIA CEMETERY

JACKSON BLVD

90

FOREST PARK

S. 1ST AVE

WALDHEIM JEWISH CEMETERY

S. WENONAH AVE

S. CENTRAL AVE

W. CERMAK RD

HARLEM AVE

55

S. HARLEM AVE

Spry picked up later that night
(6 MI. SOUTH)

63RD ST

65TH ST

OAK PARK

90

CHICAGO

55

ILLUSTRATION BY KAYLEIGH MONTGOMERY

few more minutes searching the downstairs but was careful not to wake the staff. He found nothing and left through the front door.

He jumped off the porch and edged into a nearby tree line. Duff said he felt like someone might have seen him coming out of the house. He did not know whether to go back in to find out and dispose of them or move on to where Dick was to wait in the car. He must have felt he had to go back—uncharacteristically, he'd left behind the .22 shells, and apparently hadn't wiped the floor off with a towel to literally cover his tracks, both sloppy work for a professional. Later I would read that "Oak Park officers wonder why a small caliber weapon such as a .22 pistol was used and, even more strongly, why the seven cartridge casings were left at the scene. 'The mob doesn't leave physical evidence at the scene of a hit.'"[5] But when the police found the .22 two months later they said "there was no doubt it was the tool of a professional killer."[6]

Duff continued his story. "I wasn't sure what to do, but I went back to Giancana's back porch and I listened for about five minutes and I didn't hear nothin'. I listened for a couple more minutes and thought I'd better get out of there." When he stepped off the back porch his foot hit a stony hole in the ground and he turned his ankle. He tried to take another step but quickly discovered that his knee was hurt worse than his ankle, and he reached down to grab it just as the pain hit. When he started limping to the parking lot where he was to meet Dick, he was almost sick to his stomach with the pain and it was all he could do to keep moving.

Spry wasn't there. Dick told him later that he went back to the church parking lot to wait, still covered with Giancana's blood, and hunkered down in the car. One cop car went by, and then another. Then he saw the flashing red light of a third cop car going by on a cross-street not far from the church parking lot where he was waiting. Spry was getting nervous. Now there were cop cars all over the place.

When Duff got within sight of the church lot and didn't see "nothin'," he said to himself, "Spry's wimped out and headed for the second meet-up place. I could barely walk, but I headed for Maywood, into the woods and heading north. I limped and crawled half a mile and lay down in a damn cemetery. I stayed all night. You could hear sirens all over the place, but I didn't move. One time, some cops came to the edge of the graveyard where I was and flashed their lights around for a minute or two but they didn't see me. I tried to rest, but I couldn't 'cause every time I turned over, my knee would explode with pain. Thank God it was a warm night, but still, my leg was killing me. I stopped in a park and traded clothes with a hippie."

Duff stopped telling his story long enough to take a long drink of water. When he was ready he continued. He said he gathered his strength and slipped out of the woods and picked the lock on a private home, the occupants in the upstairs bedrooms. That's the house he had called me from, trying to tell me to pick him up at Washington Park or Washington Boulevard, when I couldn't hear him. He was trying not to wake up the people upstairs. "Every time I spoke, Charley, you said, 'speak up, Duff, I can't understand you,' and dammit, Charley, I couldn't talk any louder. But you never came." I told him that I *had* come to get him, that I spent two hours looking around the Washington Park area, for nothing.

"I could hear the family starting to move around upstairs and I knew I had to get out," Duff continued, "so I slipped out the back door and kept going northwest toward the racetrack. When I got to another house I figured you'd be back home, Charley, so I broke in to call you. There was an old lady listening to the morning news on the TV upstairs, real loud." When he called me again he still had to whisper so low that I couldn't hear him. I kept asking him to 'speak up,' but he kept whispering. Now I knew why.

But it was Spry he was mad at, not me. He complained that Dick was not a stand-up guy, that he finked out on him, and that he had not waited for him with the getaway car, after Duff had put the slugs in Giancana.

By now the light in Bob's eyes was flickering again, the jolt of peace from his fix beginning to tail off. But he seemed to want to keep talking. It made sense he'd be angry with Spry for abandoning him, and in fact Dick had done so, hightailing it south on Harlem Avenue that night toward Dingess, leaving Bob to fend for himself. I would find out later that Spry was spooked once the cops showed at the church parking lot and told him to move on. Not sure what else to do, Spry headed back to West Virginia. The Summit, Illinois, police stopped Dick at 63rd Street and Harlem Avenue, he told me later. This was his second encounter with cops that night, and neither resulted in his arrest. How different my life might have been had he and Duff been caught that night.

Then Duff brought up the gun again. He complained bitterly about Dick continually asking him for money for the gun. "What the hell, Bob? I saw him with that gun back in Dingess. It was *his gun*. You owed him money for it. Nick wanted me to get you two guys together and make it right between you. You shot Dick over a few dollars? Why didn't you just pay him?" I didn't need to add that if he had, I would never have ended up in prison. Duff threw my life away over a piece of metal.

"I figured that came out of his share of the hit money. Spry was a punk," Bob hissed. It was an effort for him to maintain his anger, and his head began to shake slightly as he talked now. "Spry was a punk," he repeated, "and I couldn't risk him being alive."

"But why'd you have to do it in front of me, Bob? In my hometown?"

"'Cause he pissed me off, whining around and bitching. He was a piece of shit, Charley, and I had to ice him. I'm sorry I did it in front of you. I shoulda' shot the bastard in the woods. But I'm tellin' you, he would have ratted me out. He was a punk!" he tried to yell. The effort to raise his voice took all the strength he had at that moment. His head dropped down and a wave of pain fell on him again. His head was almost down in the bowl of cold soup in front of him.

I snapped my fingers. "Duff!" His breathing was labored, and he didn't respond. Here he was, the great killer. I was sitting across from the remnants of a man, barely breathing and holding on to the last days of a miserable life. I was still angry at Bob, but my anger was ebbing. It's hard to maintain any fury across the table from such a hollow wretch.

I sat watching Bob and waited for him to pull himself together again. I still had some questions for him.

In my anger and, frankly, curiosity about his story I let my guard down. Suddenly there was a knock at the door. I froze and reached instinctively for my .38. Bob heard it too and waved a hand with some effort. "No, no, it's OK, it's OK. It's just Jimmy Marcello. He's bringing my meds. Fa' God sake let him in. Let him in. It's OK."

I peered out the window and saw a fat man with a brown paper bag in his hand. I opened the door, and Bob made a terse introduction. Jimmy "The Man" Marcello was about five-two and 220 pounds. He shuffled in wearing wide sunglasses, a tan jacket, and a stained white golf shirt that had been too small twenty pounds ago. He had a broad pudgy face and was breathing hard from pushing his massive stomach in front of him. I'd heard of this guy, a big-time hood I was glad never to have crossed paths with.

Bob said to Jimmy, "You know where the guns are," pointing toward the hallway to his left. Jimmy returned with three guns, cradling in his arms two pump-action shotguns and a rifle. Duff was trading them for heroin. Jimmy was doing him a "favor."

Marcello sat down across from Bob, and we looked at each other. What does someone say in that situation? Hell, had there ever been a situation like that? Jimmy took the lead in making small talk, and I gradually knew the meet was over. I wasn't going to get anything more out of Bob. I stood up. "Take it easy, Bob."

"Yeah, sure, you too," he mumbled, his eyes glazing, and turned back to Jimmy.

With that I sidestepped to the door, keeping my eyes on both Duff and Marcello, making sure I wasn't going to get a slug in my back on the way out. I still kept my eye on the front door as I walked to my car, flipped the kill switch back on, and started the engine. I backed out of the driveway.

As I turned onto the main road, I reflected on the meeting with Bob. "That son of a bitch doesn't have any options. I'd probably be doing him a favor if I killed him." It looked like the cancer was going to extract a more painful revenge than I could have inflicted on him. That was OK with me. But somehow I felt cheated.

I got back to the Holiday Inn, stuffed my gear in the car, and turned east onto Route 30, toward West Virginia.

It's hard to capture how I felt, pulling away from the Heights that last time, my life with organized crime in Chicago now receding in the rearview. I knew I was lucky to be alive. I knew I might have been whacked a dozen times over. I'm almost surprised that Duff didn't turn the gun on me after he killed Spry. He was damned capable of it.

I knew I'd been both smart and lucky in my meet with Duff. I remembered how many times I was scared out of my wits when I was running with the Mob. I thought of many good guys who had been whacked or arrested and thrown into prison for long terms. Sure, the money was good. And, sure, the life was exciting, but it was also dangerous and scary. And then I remembered something else. I remembered what Joe Barrett said to me when I asked how the Outfit was doing. I remembered what he had said about how bad things had gotten, how many guys were dying in the crossfire. I'm sure had I gone back to my old work I wouldn't have lasted a year. I remembered how Barrett had told me the Mob is being pushed around, how the only guys making it big are the bosses. I'd never be one. There was nothing left for me there.

My foot pushed a little harder on the gas, and the Caddy lurched forward along Route 30. I felt lucky to be alive, and now free. I rolled down the window and smelled the pungent wind of the Chicago Heights afternoon, rolling south to a new life.

I couldn't get over it. I lost a childhood friend, my freedom, my family, and my livelihood over a hunk of metal, a simple pistol. A schoolboy's toy. I thought of Vance, my old jail mate, who had delivered that piece of metal inadvertently to Spry, thence to Duff, thence to Giancana's head. What did Spry know about the whole thing? Was there something bigger in play, some chain of events he was supposed to set running? But now he was locked away in a West Virginia prison. Why hadn't anyone pulled some strings for him? I'd never have the chance to ask him.

Then I remembered I had forgotten to ask Duff about those photos I wanted. More important, I remembered I'd forgotten to ask Duff, *What happened to the damned gun?*

18. THE PUZZLE PIECES

*I*t was still the middle of a hot afternoon when I drove away from Chicago Heights that last time, and my mind was still a jumble. I had stopped off briefly to say goodbye to Nick, since he had arranged the meet with Duff. He gave me Duff's lock picks, not that I would need them. I kept my cool, though my mind was racing as fast as my heart. I would miss Nick, who had become a father figure to me. I would never see him again. I went to St. James Hospital long enough to give Joe Barrett my best wishes for his recovery. I didn't want to stick around much longer. I got back in my car and made my way past decaying industrial plants that gradually gave way to suburbs and flat miles of nothing but Indiana. I felt I'd been holding my breath the entire time I was in the Heights. But now I had plenty of time to think.

Why should the boys around Duff have let me go? I was known for keeping my mouth shut, but now they knew I knew Duff's story. Nick couldn't protect me. Joe was in no shape to help.

But Duff's story couldn't be true, could it? At least not all of it. But much of it *had* to be true. So many of the pieces fit. At the time, I couldn't know what I didn't know, and I could get shot for asking.

It would take me years to fit the pieces of the puzzle together, as more and more details of Giancana's murder dribbled out in the press, and then gushed with the coming of the Internet. For every fact that came out there seemed to be a new theory about who killed Giancana. In none of them did all the pieces fit. But life isn't always neatly explained. I mulled it over again and again on that long drive home and to this day look for new facts that favor or disfavor Duff's account. Everything he told me about his movements that night made sense based on the years I'd spent around him. He was a master at slipping into and out of places without getting caught, a genius at picking locks, and entirely cold-blooded when given an assignment.

But if it was a hit, why would Duff also make it a robbery? He said he ransacked Giancana's place and found nothing, but I would later learn Giancana had more than $1,400 on him when the caretaker found his body around 11:30 that night.[1] Was it the drugs talking when Duff told me he turned the hit into a hit plus a robbery? Or had he reverted to the hit man's code that even if you steal you don't disturb a body, lest you leave behind some evidence? Even before the age of CSI and DNA testing, that was a well-known rule. But he did leave evidence. In one way his ransacking the place—if he did it—was consistent with the Duff I knew—thorough as a hit man but always hotheaded and looking for a little taste for himself. I could easily see him taking a little easy dough. Maybe he thought it would be neater to make it look more like a robbery than a hit. Maybe it was the junkie in him talking. Duff would never win any prizes for thinking through the morals of his jobs. He gave his employers what they wanted—did they care if he picked up a few bucks along the way? I doubted it. And Duff had a long rap sheet for burglary and robbery. Maybe old habits die hard.

Later I was able to piece together various accounts of that night, and tried to match Duff's account to them. "[A]t approximately 11:10 P.M., the body of Sam Giancana was found in the basement of his home in Oak Park, Illinois. The body was discovered by a man who described himself as the caretaker for the deceased and the home of the deceased. The caretaker and his wife lived in the house of the deceased, and the caretaker had talked to the deceased about 10:45 P.M., and at that time the deceased told him that if he needed anything he would let him know. The body was found in the kitchen area of the basement, which contains a bathroom, a laundry room, a conference-dining room and a room described as the private room of the deceased."[2] The body contained six bullet wounds in the head and neck area. "The shots had been fired at close range. In his slacks, which were unbuttoned at the top, $1,400 was found. His wallet was found on the floor between his left hand and his head. Several pieces of sausage and greens were cooking on the stove when the body was foun d."[3]

But who pulled the trigger has been the source of endless speculation. Early on it was surmised, with little supporting evidence, that it might have been a girlfriend, based on allegations that Giancana "had strange sex habits and that a .22 is a women's weapon."[4] There seems to be general agreement that the hit order came down from the top bosses at the time, Joey Aiuppa or Tony Accardo. Federal authorities said that "if the slaying was a crime syndicate execution, it could not have been carried out without going through Anthony (Big Tuna) Accardo, the mob's elder statesman. Giancana reportedly met just two weeks ago with Accardo and Joseph (Doves) Aiuppa, semi-retired Cicero rackets boss, to find out whether he was still in good standing with the mob."[5] FBI agents later said it was Aiuppa who ordered the hit on Sam.[6]

Then there's Giancana's trusted friend Butch Blasi, who was there briefly that night; Chicago researcher John Binder puts his money on Blasi, based on his being there earlier in the evening and the cops spotting his car again later that night.[7] Former FBI man William Roemer wrote an influential book pointing at Blasi as well.[8] Duff didn't mention Blasi to me. Blasi is also the favorite suspect for others, because he was the last known person to have seen Giancana alive. On the other hand, for what it's worth, Giancana's daughter and at least some quarters of the FBI don't think Blasi did it.[9]

How could I square what Duff had told me with Blasi's presence that night? Maybe Butch came in, saw the body, and wanted nothing to do with that crime scene. I have read nothing to prove or disprove Blasi's role, if any. When I go back today and review the hundreds of news stories, movies, and even plays and television treatments that cover the story of Giancana's life and death, I see scores of suppositions as to exactly who murdered him. The theories vary, but certain names keep popping up: the CIA, the Traffi- cante crime family, Joey Aiuppa, the Outfit's other crime bosses. Giancana's nephew pointed the finger at Anthony "Ant" Spilotro,[10] a view shared by "mob cop" Michael Corbitt.[11] Giancana's house seemed shockingly easy to get into and out of, and Corbitt said Spilotro "even figured out a way where he could get in through the back of Sam's place without anybody seeing him. . . . He'd go through other people's yards, go over fences, all sorts of shit."[12] If Ant could do it, believe me, Duff could.

Nick Calabrese, the son of an Outfit killer, and a made man himself, re- portedly testified as part of the "Family Secrets" trial[13] not only that Frank Sr. and Ronnie Jarrett had made the silencer for the fateful .22 Spry, Duff, and I handled but that Angelo LaPietra disposed of it, and he confirmed Tony Accardo's sanction of the hit on Giancana—none of which can be definitely confirmed. Calabrese is described by one writer as "finally coming around" and being "mostly honest" with FBI agents once he entered witness protection,[14] but in talking about Giancana he may have just been repeating stories he'd heard.

Judith Campbell Exner, intimate of Giancana, Kennedy, Sinatra, and other big names, said there's "no question" the government knocked off both Roselli and Giancana. "Things were getting too hot, what with their connection with the CIA coming out."[15]

Comparing Duff's version of events with all these speculations, nothing ruled out him pulling the trigger. The first bullet through the back of Giancana's skull would probably have killed him; six into his mouth in a "stitching pattern," sewed his mouth shut forever.[16] It was a message, not a simple hit. And Duff was a perfect courier for such messages, and it wouldn't be his first.

As for the timeline of the killing, I knew at the time, in 1975, only what I read in the papers and heard on the street. From those accounts, people seemed to be coming and going from that house on Wenonah constantly that night—the police, Giancana's friends and family, the FBI, his business associates, even his gardener. How could Duff have gotten in the front door and out again without being seen? And was no one watching the back? But as more details of that evening came to light I could see there was a large gap of time when at about 10 P.M. the police detail left to chase down a car—it turned out to belong to Sam's gardener—and drove to Accardo's house as well as that of Giancana's friend and confidante Charles "Chuckie" English, who lived in Forest Park, before returning around 10:30, but even then, despite hearing "pops" that did not sound like gunshots to them, they didn't enter the house. The cops waited until about 11:30 without entering the house despite the "pops."[17]

Although the cops would eventually say entry to the back door of the home had been barred by a steel door with a peephole, Joseph DiPersio, the caretaker, said the door was often left ajar during the summer; he didn't mention any trap door, at least not to the press.[18] DiPersio said he last shouted down to check on Giancana around 10:30 P.M. He found Giancana dead shortly after 11 P.M. but didn't call the cops until 11:53, according to his statement to the police, and newspaper accounts.[19] I could easily envision Duff pulling off the hit during that time, though he would have had to dodge the cops on his way out. Why did he go out the front door? For that matter, why did he and Spry go *in* the front door, if the back one was ajar?

Keep in mind that the details of exactly what happened that night—who came and went, at what time, why the police were withdrawn at the "right" time, why the house wasn't better guarded, whether Sam was cooking for himself or someone else have all been pieced together from various witnesses who have their own agendas, and much else rests on surmise and assumption. And a belief that the police really wanted to protect him that night, which I doubt. If the local police couldn't be trusted, how about the FBI presence on Wenonah Avenue that night? Is it possible they wanted to get rid of Giancana just as much as the Outfit did? No one could be certain who he would finger, if anyone, to the Senate panel that was to convene in just a few days. Besides the many people who wanted to use Giancana to get to other crime bosses, there were just as many, inside the government and the rotten local police, who wanted to shut him up. (After Giancana's death, his daughters went to court to suppress a search warrant to open his safe in the Wenonah house, a search local judge Daniel Covelli blocked for weeks. Once he was overruled and the safe was opened, the judge's name was found on a list showing that he had given a generous gift to Giancana's daughter at the time of her wedding.)[20] After his death the FBI said they had no jurisdiction over a state murder case, and the Chicago police said that since it happened in the suburbs it was out of their purview as well. It was absurd how quickly they all wanted to wash their hands of Giancana. The whole justice system seemed to heave a sigh of relief at his murder, and an investigation was undertaken only slowly and reluctantly.

After Giancana's death Cook County state's attorney Bernard Carey tried to investigate the murder, subpoenaing Blasi, Chuckie English, DiPersio, and others. The investigation went nowhere, because it was hampered by a lack of cooperation at the federal, state, and local levels.[21] DiPersio and others were given immunity, but the Cook County grand jury produced . . . nothing.[22] Many were obviously afraid to talk. "They won't talk because they don't like the police. That's the way they're raised, they're clannish. [T]hey seem afraid of retaliation if they do give out information."[23] A similar investigation in 1977 said it was very close to nabbing a "likely suspect" . . . and then it didn't.[24] A broadened investigation two years later also met a dead end. Giancana's estate, including his art collection and many porcelain figurines he'd collected, was auctioned off, attracting both art lovers and the morbidly curious.[25] His old house on Wenonah has become a feature on a tour of "gangster homes" in Oak Park and River Forest.[26]

Given all this, Duff's story seemed plausible. How about his account of escaping that night and being picked up the next morning by Nick and Mario? He said he went through a cemetery and then up through some woods, heading for Maywood Park Racetrack, but he never made it that far. He was picked up near Washington Park, close to Thatcher. I know that area like the back of my hand. There's a cemetery just west of Sam's house and plenty of green space just to the north of the cemetery. Duff mentioned "the Jewish cemetery," but was probably referring to Concordia. I can easily envision Duff making his way through it, bum knee and all, staying ahead of the police.

⊸ ⊸ ⊸

BUT ALL THIS knowledge was in the future. When I left Duff's house I only had his story to mull over on that long drive. I finally crossed back into West Virginia, with hundreds of miles now buffering me and my past life in the Heights. Over the next weeks and months and to this day I turn his story over in my mind. And as time has gone on I have become more and more convinced that Duff had been honest with me, to the best of his withered ability.

Only a few months after I left the Heights, one new detail revealed in the newspapers caught my eye. The gun used in Giancana's murder was found a couple of months after his murder,[27] and it was a long time after that when I got a look at it online, as a police exhibit. *But there it was, the .22, homemade silencer and all.* It was unmistakable. I'd handled it many times, the gun that cost Spry his life and me five years in the pen. The gun was found across from 135 N. Thatcher, near Thatcher and Washington in Oak Park. I made a mental map of where Duff said he'd been picked up. The gun's location matched up with his story perfectly. From there the gun became evidence, and knowing Chicago, I believe it might even have been auctioned off and is back on the streets now, or is resting in some obscure evidence locker. Or maybe some dirty cop has himself a souvenir.

As I drove I thought about all the times I had acted as chauffeur for Outfit people I knew, and many I didn't. My mind especially went back to the man I glimpsed in my rearview mirror outside the Vagabond Lounge—the one with the coldest eyes I've ever seen, and I've seen plenty. The guy Tocco told me to forget. I tried to forget it as just one more pickup, and I thought I had, until Duff told me his story. I don't think anyone could forget Johnny Roselli, Handsome Johnny, and I believed Duff more when he mentioned Tocco. The night I drove Roselli to the meet must have been when the whole thing was laid out. Roselli's motive? There are many theories. It is reported that he and Giancana were intimately involved with CIA efforts in the early 1960s to assassinate Fidel Castro; the Cuban dictator cost Giancana a lot of money when he came to power and forced the gangsters off the island.[28] Roselli was also linked to the Kennedy assassination. I did note that Roselli was called to testify before the Senate Intelligence Committee less than a year after Giancana's death, but apparently he didn't tell them enough to blow the lid off the whole CIA/Mob/Kennedy connection publicly . . . or maybe he told them just enough to get himself killed.[29] Maybe the truth, like Roselli himself, has been sawed up and dropped in the ocean, or left to molder in the same nether land where people like Jimmy Hoffa lie.

I GOT OUT of the car back home that day, utterly weary but safe enough in West Virginia, and knew I couldn't spread any of this around. Not yet. Even asking questions about it might be enough to pull me back into the life I have worked hard since 1980 to escape. But I kept notes and read newspapers, and when the Internet came along I learned just enough to do my own research. I also talked by phone quietly with a few Heights people from time to time.

For years Uncle Columbus and then the noncoms of the Outfit were my substitute family, and all families have secrets. Sometimes, as one generation passes on, the secrets turn into old news and eventually into legends. Rumors and stories and outright lies pile up like sticks behind a dam. Except for that West Virginia golf course when I was ten, my path never physically crossed Sam Giancana's, but my life seems somehow tied up with his. I've spent the rest of my life getting out from under his accidental influence on my life. Fate threw me into the Heights but let me leave it again.

After all this time and all the details that have dribbled out, do I still believe Duff's story? There are days I wonder, but yes, I do believe it, at least in the particular that matters, and that's probably why you picked up this book: I believe Duff pulled the trigger, and the order came from Roselli via Tocco, with Accardo's assent, and the gun came from Vance, and it cost my friend Dick Spry his life. I believe the cops found the gun exactly where Duff dropped it.

Does everything in his story tie up neatly? No, but in life, as in the legend, now, of Sam Giancana, not everything does.

EPILOGUE: FROM THE MOB TO THE MINES

So that's my story. Judge me as you will. In the years that followed, money was tight and friends few, and I considered, only briefly, going back to the Heights. Maybe I could get back to the horses. Those thoughts came and went. I realized that the life expectancy of a Mob member was far lower than the biblical three score and ten. I can name over a dozen guys I personally worked with who met untimely ends—good, loyal guys, too.

NICK D'ANDREA WOULD live less than a year after I last saw him, gunned down, according to a judge, by the same Jimmy Marcello I saw on my last trip to the Heights, the same guy who "helped" Duff score his heroin by buying his guns.[1] Marcello is languishing in prison as of this writing. The "body of the then-49-year-old D'Andrea, of Chicago Heights, was discovered Sept. 13, 1981, in the trunk of his burned out Mercedes-Benz two miles east of Crete."[2] It was speculated that "Nicholas D'Andrea was killed in connection with the attempted assassination of south suburban mob boss Alfred Pilotto, who was shot while playing golf with his brother, Henry, in July 1981. Henry Pilotto was at the time the police chief in Chicago Heights. Both Pilottos survived the shooting attempt."[3] Nick's brother Mario, then forty-two, soon followed Nick; according to the official story he "was killed by federal agents during an undercover drug buy in October 1981 after Mario D'Andrea allegedly pulled a gun when an undercover Drug Enforcement Administration officer identified himself."[4] Of course, there is always an official story and then there's the real story; some believe the takeout of Mario was more like a legally sanctioned hit than a matter of self-defense. Nick and Mario had to die, while the Pilottos got to live. But that's a story for someone else to write.

Joe Barrett continued to run the new Vagabond, showing up later in newspaper accounts of police busts for running a house of prostitution.

The location of the old Vagabond Lounge, the Flatiron Building, was added to the National Register of Historic Places in 2003, and then torn down in 2009, despite efforts to preserve it.

I've got a feeling Roland Vance, "Mr. Lucky," the ultimate source of the gun Duff used on Giancana—ironically, a gun lost by Vance in a card game—knew more about the whole thing than any of us, and took it with him to the grave at the state prison in Moundsville, apparently shanked by another inmate.

Tocco's "luck" and protection would hold until 1989, when he was finally convicted of dozens of felonies.[5]

Uncle Columbus would play less and less of a role in my life as I got older and took on my own obligations with the Outfit. I rarely saw him, and he would die soon after I got out of prison.

After our meeting Duff would linger for just a few days before the cancer took him. Not long before my last encounter with him, he was featured in a newspaper article about inmates at Statesville prison selling their original artwork. The newspaper singled him out by name: "Robert Zazzetti 'charmed the kids'" with his paintings of Walt Disney characters.[6] He was sick with cancer even then, so once again he was out on the streets, soon turning into the mess I last saw. I still get chills when I think of him "charming" anyone.

The crazy world I was thrust into as a teen has only gotten crazier, even if the more apparent influence of the Outfit has waned and some of the top men, and bought-off judges and lawyers, have gone to prison or died.

AFTER I LEFT jail I had a long hill before me. I needed to find an honest way to make a living and to find a peaceful home, and I hoped, against all odds, to reconnect with the four children who had been whisked away from me. My wife had, understandably, liquidated my assets when I was sentenced—after all, she had four mouths to feed.

When I had done my time I needed a job. I was still good with cars and was a quick study; maybe I could make something of that. In the West Virginia prison work release program, I had worked on Beckley's fleet of police cruisers, keeping every one clean, shiny, and smooth-running. I had no grand plan, but looking back I think it's obvious the first phase of my transition to be a responsible man took place in the prison work program, where I maintained all those cars. Even the state police came to recognize my skills. I was living a normal life in an apartment and working an eight-to-five job. When my work release was over it was time to get on with the rest of my life.

I was always a bit of a brawler. I had to be. I'm not a big man, and nothing was given to me when I was a kid. Everything was a fight, and my little town was full of bullies, little men as little boys, whose only success in life would be to take something someone else had worked hard for. In that way, I thought ironically, they were little different from the Outfit bosses. I didn't know my early brawling would be superior training for how to deal with the petty hoods in the Outfit or to intimidate business owners for the street tax. But the skills I learned in defending myself were valuable offensive weapons to the Outfit. It's to my everlasting shame that in learning to beat bullies I became one. Oh, I told myself that it was just something that had to be done. Still, too many of the dollars I pocketed were really someone else's. I won't share some of the roles I played, first because I'm not proud of them and second because who knows who will read this? There could still be some prosecutor out there ready to call me to account.

And old habits die hard. In the years after I said goodbye to the Heights I often took two steps forward and one back. A little too much liquor, a little too much mouth. But there was a center line I was determined to find.

Once I was free I decided that if I was going to stay in West Virginia, coal would have to pay my bills. I bought a very small, failing mine with terrible labor problems and turned it into a mine that could be sold at a profit, which I did. I was ambitious, so I started a new mine from scratch in a nonunion environment and made a success of it as well. Then, unlike most mine owners in the boom-and-bust of West Virginia, I knew when to get out, and I did.

The things I learned along the way in the coal industry could make a book themselves. Suffice it to say that while not as blatant as in Chicago, the powers that really control things are watching every moment. The players are different, the game is the same.

I have to admit that I miss the reputation of being, for all practical purposes, a "made man," a respected and protected man of the mob. Don't we all want to be known? "That's Charley Hager. You don't mess with him." Few people who think this way know the price that comes with it.

-•- -•- -•-

I LEFT THE impression above that I was through with Chicago (or maybe it was through with me). That's not quite the truth. I went there once to see my wife's sister. Since she still lived in the same house, I had no trouble finding her. She and I and her husband had always gotten along really well, so I felt comfortable going there. She greeted me at the door with a big hug. "Let me fix you a cup of coffee," she said, and I followed her to the kitchen; she pulled out a chair for me, and we exchanged "remember-whens" for about half an hour before I got to the point of my visit.

"I guess you know why I'm here. I need to find my wife and my children."

How I would know that she knew where to find them will remain my secret.

"I expected you'd want to find them," she replied, quietly, "but, if I tell you, you have to promise me, *give me your word that you won't hurt her,* and you won't hurt the man she's married to now, or the children. Promise me, Charley."

I had already come to that conclusion. I just wanted to be the best kind of father I could, whatever that was, given the circumstances. How many guys were in this position, given any kind of second chance? Certainly not Dick. Not the miserable Bob Duff, aka Robert Zazzetti, aka I wish I'd never laid eyes on him. But our lives were stitched together as surely as my mother's old quilt, the three of us. I sensed some cycle at work here, a generational malady that I was determined to cure. I loved my kids and needed to be the father for them that I'd never had.

"Of course I'm not going to hurt her. She's the mother of my children. And I won't hurt her husband. I hope she's made a better life than I gave her." In my mind I said "unless he keeps me from seeing my kids."

She scribbled a few lines on the top sheet of a notepad and handed it to me. "Here you are, Charley. I'm giving it to you with my love and my trust. I'm not wild about Sally. We're very different people, but I couldn't stand to see something happen to her." She picked up the coffee cups and put them in the sink.

I thanked her, and we said our goodbyes. I would never see her again.

The following May I locked up my apartment and headed south to Charlotte, North Carolina. After killing the engine, I looked up from the street at a small house and had just a little anxiety, wondering how the next hour or so would pass. Finally, I thought to myself, "Here we go!" I shoved open the door and headed up the driveway.

In the next few hours I received a gift, one unearned but welcome: I re-connected with my children, I made a separate peace with my ex-wife. Well, that didn't go so bad, I thought to myself as I left. Not bad at all.

I headed north again. As I started seeing the signs for Beckley, I looked above the steep West Virginia mountains and saw one lonely star. I hoped it was a Charley Hager star—a lucky star that would bring some order and make some sense out of my twisting and turning life.

In time I would meet, woo, and marry a nurse. I opened a small business and traded it for a larger. I shut that down. I quit drinking. I made investments. I made notes for this book. I found a nice house with a big yard. I spent time with my kids. I'm satisfied that, given the hand I was dealt, I've played it as best I could.

Nothing good seems to last in the life of a criminal; the lucky ones just have long runs of good fortune and hope there's no bullet waiting at the end of the ride. I had my horses for only a little more than three years, but I miss them. Now that I've gone straight, I have to admit I miss some of the big money and the excitement of the Mob. I don't miss, however, the chance that you might get killed. But I really miss those horses. In the wee hours of the morning, in the half-sleep of dreams, I'm back in the seat of a sulky with my feet pushing hard and the reins and whip in my hand, speeding along close to the ground at thirty or forty miles an hour.

I have only a few mementos left from those days in the Heights. Every now and then, however, I get out Duff's set of lock picks and jingle them, just to remind myself that although I left Chicago, I can't forget the lessons it taught me.

AFTERWORD / ACKNOWLEDGMENTS
NOTES / INDEX

AFTERWORD

I became interested in the era of Chicago crime history that Charley describes here because my great-uncles, Nick and Mario and their brothers, lived it. They are major players in the story you just read. I was not alive for any of this and can only speak from what I have read, heard, been told, or studied. In college I was asked to research Chicago gang history, particularly my family history alongside political corruption in the Chicago area. The research was both primary and secondary. At the University of Illinois at Chicago (UIC), criminal justice professor John Hagedorn selected me for the Liberal Arts and Sciences Undergraduate Research Initiative (LASURI) in 2008–9. The Family Secrets trial was then making national headlines, and my cousin Bobby D'Andrea, Nick's son, was in pursuit of justice. He was nineteen years old in 1981, when his father was murdered, and just two weeks later Bobby was at his uncle Mario's gas station when Mario was gunned down by the Drug Enforcement Administration. Bobby was taken into custody and held for three days without charge, bail, or bond. What happened to him is infuriating. Bobby and I talked every day during the Family Secrets trial, and he helped me look into our own family's secrets. When anyone came to me with questions I turned to Bobby for answers. Much of what I wrote and spoke were Bobby's words. My actions were his; he was my motive.

I could not let the injustice of it all go unsaid and became obsessed with looking into politicians and government employees who were working with organized criminals throughout Chicago history. I remember the words of Professor Hagedorn when he was conducting interviews for the LASURI selection at UIC. Hagedorn had studied gang history in over a dozen nations. He chose to work at UIC to take a closer look at Chicago.

"Why do you think organized crime is so successful here in Chicago?" he asked. I responded, "Political corruption." Then Hagedorn asked, "Why are political corruption and organized crime more prevalent throughout the history of Chicago than anywhere else in the U.S.?" I responded with one word: "Family." Bobby and I started looking into anyone suspicious in his past after that. This is the sole reason I became familiar with the Italian Mafia and what later became the Italian Mob.

When I was approached and asked to write an essay for Charley's manuscript I immediately gave the manuscript to Bobby. It turned out to be the last piece of writing I brought to him to review. It is rare that an author would seek out a D'Andrea opinion, and even rarer that Bobby liked what he read on these matters. This manuscript was the first and last on the subject that he would express favor in to me. Bobby agreed to write a foreword for Charley's manuscript and discussed meeting with Charley to go over it. Bobby said it was good, though some of it was incredible. Bobby professionally built and raced cars his whole life, and the plan was that he and Charley would talk further when racing season was over. But it was not to be. Bobby had a heart attack while working on a car, passing away October 7, 2016.

Many things we were able to move on from. Others had an irreversible effect. For the last time I will speak on behalf of Bobby, as I have in the past, and I vow to finish all he and I have started. Charley's book is one that we believe in. We wish Charley all the best in life, appreciate the opportunity of input, and stand beside his story with full support. May Robert Joseph D'Andrea rest in peace. He will live forever in our hearts and in the fraction of an instant that a vehicle dances in air; "Godspeed."

Ashleigh D'Andrea

ACKNOWLEDGMENTS

Among the many people who helped put this book together, those whose kind assistance we especially appreciate are Barbara Hager, Margot van Eck, Warren H. Anderson, Louis Corsino, Thurman Miller, John Hagedorn, Rich Lindberg, John Binder, John Lynch, Ashleigh D'Andrea, Yuval Taylor, Robert Lombardo, Sylvia Frank Rodrigue, Kayleigh Montgomery, Matthew Luzi, Sally Watts, Amy J. Etcheson, Karl Kageff, Joe Anthony, Judy Verdich, Ben Gibson, Derek Krissoff, Michael Mattis, Alice Speilburg, Claudia Ellis, Constantine D. Vasilios and Associates, Ltd., and David Beal.

Bob Dylan epigraph courtesy Dwarf Music, copyright 1966, renewed 1994. Used by permission.

Map courtesy of Kayleigh Montgomery; © 2017 Charles Hager and David T. Miller.

NOTES

Prologue

1. Early accounts of the killing, such as "Sam Giancana Found Slain," *Spokane Daily Chronicle*, June 20, 1976, 42, were soon supplemented with more exhaustive articles, for example, William Brashler, "The Death of a 'Godfather,'" *New York Magazine*, July 28, 1975, 27.

2. The 1960s were a fertile time for someone like Columbus to bring someone like me along. The long history of the Outfit is far beyond this book, but for an exhaustive account of its rise and how it differed from the Mafia, see John Binder, *The Chicago Outfit* (Chicago: Arcadia, 2003); and Louis Corsino, *The Neighborhood Outfit: Organized Crime in Chicago Heights* (Champaign: University of Illinois Press, 2014). Matthew Luzi's *The Boys in Chicago Heights: The Forgotten Crew of the Chicago Outfit* (Chicago: University of Illinois Press, 2012) is also essential reading about this time period. For crime in Chicago proper, see Robert M. Lombardo, *Organized Crime in Chicago: Beyond the Mafia* (Chicago: University of Illinois Press, 2013), http://www.jstor.org/stable/10.5406/j.ctt2tt9mc.

1. Triply Damned

1. "[I]f one were to choose those states whose politics (excluding the baroque courthouse states of the South) are the most squalid, corrupt and despicable, then one would add West Virginia to that Jukes family of American politics that includes Indiana, Massachusetts and Texas. . . . Politics in West Virginia involves money—hot money, under-the-table money, open money." Theodore H. White, *The Making of the President, 1960* (Harper Collins, paperback edition, 2009), 97–99.

2. Rick Steelhammer, "Planned Rehab Project Should Extend Life of 124-Year-Old Mingo Tunnel," *Charleston Gazette Mail*, September 5, 2016, accessed July 3, 2017, http://www.wvgazettemail.com/news/20160905/planned-rehab-project-should-extend-life-of-124-year-old-mingo-tunnel.

3. Any thought that this area's influence is purely historical is misplaced. Dingess produced a native son governor, Okey L. Patteson, and West Virginia's current governor, Earl Ray Tomblin, is from nearby Logan County.

2. CHICAGO, UNCLE COLUMBUS, AND A NEW LIFE

1. Mingo County has long had the distinction of being among the most corrupt and violent areas in the country. "If there are more corrupt places in the United States than Williamson and surrounding Mingo County, the embarrassed and stunned residents of this achingly poor coal community will gladly surrender their notoriety." B. Drummond Ayres Jr., "Corruption Inquiry Brings Hope to 'Bloody Mingo,'" *New York Times*, March 25, 1988, accessed June 10, 2017, http://www.nytimes.com/1988/03/25/us/corruption-inquiry-brings-hope-to-bloody-mingo.html; "Almost Heaven? This Corrupt Corner of West Virginia Was More Like the Other Place," *People Magazine*, November 14, 1988, accessed April 30, 2017, http://people.com/archive/almost-heaven-this-corrupt-corner-of-west-virginia-was-more-like-the-other-place-vol-30-no-20/.

4. CLOTHES MAKE THE BOY

1. It would be another ten years before "chop shops," where stolen cars were broken down and parted out, became commonplace in Chicago. Once they did, a new round of gang rivalry was set off and referred to as the "chop shop wars." See Scott Burnstein, "The Chop-Shop Wars: Mafia in Chicago Assumed Control of Car-Theft Industry in Brutal Fashion," *Gangster Report*, accessed June 9, 2017, http://gangsterreport.com/the-chop-shop-wars-mafia-in-chicago-assumed-control-of-car-theft-industry-in-bloody-fashion/, for a summary of the many hits associated with this era.

2. Corsino explores the Outfit's Italian origins in *The Neighborhood Outfit.*

3. But I'm not saying this was true for the Outfit in general—its involvement in the narcotics trade goes back to the Capone era, as John J. Binder shows in *Al Capone's Beer Wars: A Complete History of Organized Crime in Chicago during Prohibition* (Amherst, NY: Prometheus Books, 2017).

4. At least when I was there, street crews didn't target innocent people. As one member put it, "The Outfit guys never bothered anybody except their own. If you'd cross them, they would take care of you. But as far as hurting innocent people, that just never happened. You could even say they protected the neighborhood. Nobody came on Taylor Street to do robberies or to break into houses—they'd be dead if they tried anything like that. We didn't have to lock our doors or windows; the Outfit made us feel safe. And from Capone's days till now, you know, the Syndicate has been known to help people out with hospital bills and whatnot. It burns me up when I see police picking on them and letting the real crooks go free." Quoting a Taylor Street resident, interview respondent 24, 1994, in Lombardo, *Organized Crime in Chicago*, 206 n. 20.

5. Don Babwin, "Trial Shows Mob Aging but Still Around," *Washington Post,* August 25, 2007, accessed April 30, 2017, http://www.washingtonpost.com /wp-dyn/content/article/2007/08/25/AR2007082500744_pf.html.

5. HOME AGAIN

1. Opinion, case no. 20978, *In the Matter of J. Ned Grubb, Judge, Circuit Court of Logan County,* Supreme Court of Appeals of West Virginia, April 7, 1992, accessed July 3, 2017, http://www.courtswv.gov/supreme-court/docs/spring1992/20978 .htm.

6. AN UNMADE MAN

1. "Organized Crime to Folk and People Street Gangs," *Chicago Gang History,* September 2, 2016, http://chicagoganghistory.com/mob-influence-modern -gang/, accessed June 11, 2017.

2. For more on Accardo, see William Roemer, *Accardo: The Genuine Godfather* (New York: Donald I. Fine, 1995).

3. The 1950s brought new leadership to the Capone syndicate. Things were changing. The old-timers who had known Al Capone were dead, in prison, or living in lavish suburban homes, and a new group of younger men was taking their place. These new gangsters weren't born in Sicily, nor did they grow up running beer during Prohibition. They were former delinquents who had terrorized the streets of Chicago's river wards. Among them were many members of the Forty-two Gang. The entrance of the Forty-two Gang had marked a turning point in organized crime in Chicago.
Lombardo, *Organized Crime in Chicago,* 119.

4. Kitty Kelley, "Nobody but Nobody Messed with Frank," *Sydney (Australia) Morning Herald,* September 10, 1986.

5. Bryan Smith, "How the CIA Enlisted the Chicago Mob to Put a Hit on Castro," *Chicago Magazine,* October 23, 2007, accessed June 11, 2017, http:// www.chicagomag.com/Chicago-Magazine/November-2007/How-the-CIA -Enlisted-the-Chicago-Mob-to-Put-a-Hit-on-Castro/; Select Committee to Study Governmental Operations with Respect to Intelligence Activities, Alleged Assassination Plots Involving Foreign Leaders (Washington, DC: U.S. Government Printing Office, 1975), Wikimedia Commons, https://commons .wikimedia.org/wiki/File%3ASenate_Report_No._94-465_(1975).pdf, accessed October 6, 2017.

6. Sandy Smith quoted in Bob Greene, "In Chicago: New Syndicate 'King' More Ruthless Than Capone," *Cincinnati Enquirer,* May 12, 1963, 10.

7. Nicholas Gage, "Giancana Boxed In Several Times, but 'Feds' Let Him Out," *Winona (Minn.) Daily News*, June 13, 1976, 18.

8. Sandy Smith, "How FBI Exposed 12-Headed Gang Monster," *Akron (Ohio) Beacon-Journal*, September 1, 1963, 3.

9. Thomas Powers, "Giancana to Include Sheriff in U.S. Suit," *Chicago Tribune*, July 18, 1963; Nicholas Gage, "U.S. Dogged Giancana, but Then Let Him Off," *Long Beach (Calif.) Independent*, April 13, 1976, 16.

10. "Silent Sam Giancana Wears Loud Clothes," *Asbury Park (New Jersey) Press*, September 13, 1963, 3.

11. Gage, "Giancana Boxed In," 18.

12. Kitty Kelley, "Sinatra-JFK, Fast Friends, Fast Times," *Jackson (Tenn.) Sun*, October 16, 1986, 13. On the other hand, Peter Lawford described him as "an awful guy with a gargoyle face and weasel nose," quoted in Kitty Kelley, "Nobody but Nobody." "Silent Sam" was said to have two sides, the flamboyant Cosa Nostra kingpin and "a playboy who is fond of fun and games, like silk suits and night clubs, and sports a red cap on the golf course." He "alternately smirked and frowned" when he testified before a Senate committee in 1959; "Silent Sam Giancana Wears Loud Clothes," 3.

13. Quoted in Kelley, "Sinatra-JFK."

14. William Hundley, chief of the Department of Justice's organized crime section under Bobby Kennedy said, "Bobby pushed to get Giancana at any cost"; quoted in Gage, "U.S. Dogged Giancana, 16.

15. Quoted in Ronald Koziol, "U.S. Agents Look Again at Mob Hits," *Chicago Tribune*, December 12, 1988, accessed July 3, 2017, http://articles.chicagotribune.com/1988-12-12/news/8802230757_1_mob-boss-mob-hits-crime-syndicate.

16. Koziol, "U.S. Agents Look Again."

17. "Giancana Lost Grip in Jail, Judge Reports," *Chicago Tribune*, April 27, 1967, 4.

18. "New Life Style Adopted by Mobster Gone Mod," *Pottstown (Pennsylvania) Mercury*, November 29, 1972, 16.

19. The 1960s in Chicago might be seen as a classic case study of competing pressures on street organizations from revolutionary politics and the rackets. Revolutionary groups, like the Black Panthers and Young Lords, competed with the gangs for the allegiance of street youth. At the same time, the new black gangs took control of the drug traffic and other underground services and permanently displaced the Italian Outfit. . . . Martin Luther King met with Vice Lords at the beginning of his Chicago open housing campaign. This rapprochement of the gangs and civil rights organizations was viewed

as a major threat by the city machine and federal authorities, who used both over violence and covert means to sow discord between the two [citations omitted].

Gangs in the Global City: Alternatives to Traditional Criminology, edited by John M. Hagedorn (Champaign: University of Illinois Press, 2007), 22.

    20. Binder, *Chicago Outfit,* 89.

7. A License to Steal

    1. The Vagabond is referenced in "Ex-Wife Casts Doubt over Photo ID," *Chicago Tribune,* July 25, 2007, 8.

    2. For example, "Tony D'Andrea Assassinated," *The Chicago Crime Scenes Project,* October 17, 2009, accessed June 11, 2017, http://chicagocrimescenes.blogspot.com/2009/10/tony-dandrea-assassinated.html, tells the story of the 1921 hit on Anthony D'Andrea.

    3. The top leadership of the Chicago Outfit has historically been referred to as the West Side. Most of the bosses after Al Capone lived in a western suburb; hence the term *West Side* referred to the top leadership of the mob. When gangsters had to see the top guys, they would have to "see the guy out west." The term *West Side,* when used to refer to the hierarchy of the Outfit, also refers to the fact that organized crime in Chicago has been dominated by the Taylor Street Crew since the 1950s and the emergence of the Outfit as we know it today.

Lombardo, *Organized Crime in Chicago,* 192 (citations omitted).

    4. John O'Connell, "A Tale Told through Terra Cotta: Chicago Heights Preservationists See the Past in Flat Iron Building," *NWI Times,* May 31, 2001, accessed May 1, 2017, http://www.nwitimes.com/uncategorized/a-tale-told-through-terra-cotta/article_1a880e70-874f-5fee-b047-99d8cb4465ce.html.

8. The Ropes

    1. Henry Wood, "Mob Rules Broken—Violator Pays the Price," *Chicago Tribune,* August 9, 1972, 1, accessed June 12, 2017, http://archives.chicagotribune.com/1972/08/09/page/1/article/front-page-1-no-title.

10. Mr. Lucky

    1. "If His Luck Holds," *Traverse City (Mich.) Record Eagle,* January 2, 1973, 6.

    2. Sean Toolan, "Prisoners Profit by Brush with Society," *Chicago Tribune,* August 13, 1979, sec. 4, 1.

    3. "Man Is Found Guilty on Ogle Burglary Case," *Freeport (Ill.) Journal-Standard,* March 10, 1961, 3.

4. "Hold 3 in Drug Store Robberies," *Mt. Vernon (Ill.) Register-News*, September 17, 1963, 2.

5. "Ogle Jury Returns Indictments," *Dixon (Ill.) Evening Telegraph*, March 29, 1963, 4.

6. "Two Charged in Motel Theft," *Southern Illinoisan (Carbondale)*, December 3, 1968, 2.

7. See, for example, *People v. Zazzetti*, 286 N.E.2d 745 (Ill. App. Ct. 1972), accessed June 12, 2017, Appellate Court of Illinois, https://www.courtlistener.com/opinion/2226280/people-v-zazzetti/.

8. *People v. Zazzetti*, 69 Ill. App.3d 588 (Ill. App. Ct. 1979), accessed April 30, 2017, https://casetext.com/case/people-v-zazzetti-1.

9. Jeff Coen, "Hit Man's Son Takes Stand; Witness Backs Mobster's Brother," *Chicago Tribune*, July 25, 2007, accessed July 15, 2017, http://articles.chicagotribune.com/2007-07-25/news/0707241079_1_gambling-operation-nicholas-calabrese-chicago-outfit; Jeff Coen, "Mobster Gets Life Term," *Chicago Tribune*, February 6, 2009, accessed April 30, 2017, http://www.chicagotribune.com/news/local/breaking/ch-090206-secrets-story.html.

10. Frank Calabrese Jr., Keith Zimmerman, Kent Zimmerman, and Paul Pompian, *Operation Family Secrets: How a Mobster's Son and the FBI Brought Down Chicago's Murderous Crime Family* (New York: Broadway Books, 2012).

11. "Widow: Hubby Drove Mercedes to His Death," *Northwest Herald* (Woodstock, Ill.), July 25, 2007, 4C.

12. John O'Brien, "Mob Violence: Bullets Riddle Hit Man, Wife," *Chicago Tribune*, July 3, 1980, sec. 1, 1. John Kass, "FBI Dusts Off Old, Cold Case of Hit on Hit-Man," *Chicago Tribune*, July 2, 2004, sec. 1, 2; http://articles.chicagotribune.com/2004-07-02/news/0407020095_1_coffee-shop-van-car.

13. *Roland Vance v. Jerry C. Hedrick, Acting Warden Harley Mooney, Superintendent, West Virginia State Police*, 659 F.2d 447 (4th Cir. 1981), accessed July 2, 2017, https://www.courtlistener.com/opinion/394098/roland-vance-v-jerry-c-hedrick-acting-warden-harley-mooney/.

11. A PUNK IN THE TRUNK

1. Fred Pascente and Sam Reaves, *Mob Cop: My Life of Crime in the Chicago Police Department* (Chicago: Chicago Review Press 2015), 60.

2. Informants report that members of the Chicago Outfit never use the terms soldier, capo or consigliere. . . . There is a definite distinction between being a made guy and being a worker within the Chicago Outfit. To be a made guy, one has to be a boss or a person of special status within the organization, and not just a member. The head of the Outfit and his advisors are made guys. The heads of the street crews

and their 'lieutenants,' persons with a definite area of responsibility, are also said to be made guys. Being a made guy grants certain rights and privileges that other members do not have. Made guys manage the operations, give orders, and profit more than everybody else. Becoming the boss of a crew is a good indication that the member has been "made." Associating with made guys and assuming responsibility within the organization is also an indication of who is likely to be a made guy. To be a made guy one also has to be Italian, and not just any kind of Italian, but southern Italian, Neapolitan, or Sicilian. Some non-Italians carry great stature within the Outfit because of their advanced age or accomplishments within the organization, but they are not made guys.

Lombardo, *Organized Crime in Chicago*, 155–56 (citations omitted).

12. I'm the Guy

1. For a summary of Roselli's long and infamous career and his gruesome demise, see Sifakis, *The Mafia Encyclopedia* (Infobase Publishing, 2006), 392–93.

2. Michael J. Goodman, "Spilotro Seizes 'Mickey Mouse Mafia,'" *Los Angeles Times*, February 25, 1983, 1.

3. For more on the election see Gus Russo, *The Outfit: The Role of Chicago's Underworld in the Shaping of Modern America* (New York: Bloomsbury, 2001), 374; F. James Davis, *West Virginia Tough Boys: Vote Buying, Fist Fighting, and a President Named JFK* (Chapmanville, WV: Woodland Press, 2003).

4. Kitty Kelley, "Nobody but Nobody Messed with Frank," *Sydney (Australia) Morning Herald*, September 10, 1986, 17.

5. Before the crucial state primary election Ellis is reported to have received $50,000 from Kennedy's team, Ellis supposedly saying Kennedy didn't buy West Virginia, he "just rented it for the day." Thomas J. Craughwell, *Presidential Payola: The True Story of Monetary Scandals in the Oval Office* (Fair Winds Press, 2011), 102. For a vivid account of the shifting loyalties in the 1960 primary, based on interviews with many of West Virginia's elite political fixers, see Davis, *West Virginia Tough Boys*. On the other hand, Ellis says Kennedy was popular in the area and "[a] lot of the national magazines moved in here during the primary. They attended some of the campaign meetings, and left here with all types of stories, some true and some not, about how the people worked here. They left with the story that Kennedy had enough money to buy West Virginia or Logan County. But in the case of Logan County he didn't have to buy it. The people went for him here; he spent very little money here in this area." Claude Ellis interview, September 9, 1964, John F. Kennedy Library, https://archive2.jfklibrary.org/JFKOH/Ellis,%20Claude/JFKOH-CE-01/JFKOH-CE-01-TR.pdf.

6. Giancana apparently didn't foresee Kennedy's appointing his brother Bobby as attorney general to take down organized crime. "[H]istory would have been different without the Outfit's participation in in the 1960 election: 'Nixon would have been elected. No assassinations, no Watergate, and most important to the Outfit, no Bobby Kennedy as Attorney General. The history of the United States from 1960 'til eternity was made by a mobster from Chicago's West Side who wanted to impress a crooner from New Jersey.'" Russo, *The Outfit*, 403.

7. *Alleged Assassination Plots Involving Foreign Leaders* (Washington, DC: U.S Government Printing Office), Wikimedia Commons, https://commons.wikimedia .org/wiki/File%3ASenate_Report_No._94-465_(1975).pdf.

8. Michael O'Brien, "The Exner File: Truth and Fantasy from a President's Mistress," *Washington Monthly*, December 1999, http://www.unz.org/Pub /WashingtonMonthly-1999dec-00036, accessed November 29, 2017.

9. "Marilyn Monroe 'Spent Her Last Night with Mafia Boss Sam Giancana at Frank Sinatra's Lodge,'" *Daily Mail*, April 29, 2011, http://www.dailymail.co.uk /news/article-1381431/Marilyn-Monroe-spent-night-mafia-boss-Sam-Giancana -Frank-Sinatras-lodge.html.

10. "Reputed Crime Leader Jailed in Inquiry," *Anderson (Ind.) Herald*, June 2, 1965, 2.

11. "Judge Again Slaps Court on Giancana," *Orlando (Fla.) Sentinel*, June 3, 1966, 6; "A Defeat for Law and Order," editorial, *Chicago Tribune*, June 2, 1966, 18.

12. "Mob May Replace Giancana," *Chicago Tribune*, June 5, 1966, 2.

13. Peter F. Vaira, chief of the Justice Department Strike Force against organized crime, quoted in "Slain Chicago Mobster Giancana Said 'I Steal,'" *Indianapolis Star*, June 21, 1975, 8. Senator Frank Church, chair of the committee investigating the CIA, said the CIA would have had no motive to kill Giancana, since the committee "already is in possession of the facts and 'we have other sources.'" Ibid.

14. "Inquiry Had Planned to Call Giancana," *New York Times*, June 21, 1975, 12; Weldon Whisler and John O'Brien, "Cops Watching Home Night Giancana Slain," *Chicago Sun-Times*, June 21, 1975, 1. The killer "may have passed directly under the gaze of lawmen."

15. Lee Winfrey, "A Gangster and Singer in Love," *Philadelphia Inquirer*, November 25, 1995, 56.

13. GOODBYE SAM, GOODBYE DICK

1. According to *New York Magazine*, the unit followed a car that left Giancana's home just after 10 P.M. but lost it in traffic, then drove to Chuck English's home and Tony Accardo's house in River Forest, the next village over from Oak Park,

before returning to Giancana's at about ten thirty. William Brashler, "The Death of a 'Godfather,'" *New York Magazine,* July 28, 1975, 32.

2. "Nab Two Illinois Men in Murder in W. Virginia," *Mt. Vernon (Ill.) Register-News,* October 2, 1975, 10.

3. "Illinois Man Charged with Murder Refuses Extradition," *Charleston (W.Va.) Daily Mail,* October 3, 1975, 3.

14. WITH FRESH EYES

1. Racketeer Influenced and Corrupt Organizations Act (RICO), Title IX of the Organized Crime Control Act of 1970, Pub. L. No. 91–452, 84 Stat. 941 (Oct. 15, 1970), codified at 18 U.S.C. Ch. 96, §§1961–1968.

2. John O'Brien, "Mob Slaying May Be Signal," *Chicago Tribune,* October 5, 1981, http://archives.chicagotribune.com/1981/10/05/page/19/article/mob-slaying-may-be-signal.

3. Liam Ford, "Musings, Murders, Morals: Tapes of Reputed Mobster Depict Life in Outfit," *Chicago Tribune,* July 11, 2007, sec. 2, 1.

4. Robert Lombardo suggests,

> Organized crime activity in the Chicago Heights community has ended. The 1989 conviction of Chicago Heights mob boss Albert Tocco was devastating to the Chicago Heights Street Crew. The card rooms and social clubs are gone, and it is now difficult to locate organized crime figures in the Chicago Heights area. However, the influence of the Chicago Heights Crew was felt as recently as 1992 when Chicago Heights mayor Charles Panici and two former city councilmen were indicted for extorting money from numerous contractors who wanted to do business with the city. Among the contractors who gave money to the mayor was crime boss Albert Tocco, who also held the city's garbage hauling contract. . . . The decline of the Chicago Heights Crew has coincided with other changes that have taken place in the community. The post–World War II period saw the creation of new suburban areas and the development of regional shopping centers that hastened the end of Chicago Heights' once bustling downtown business district. In addition, the decline of the railroads and the demise of heavy industry in the area have added to the deterioration of the town."

Robert M. Lombardo, *Organized Crime in Chicago: Beyond the Mafia* (Urbana: University of Illinois Press, 2013), 185 (citations omitted).

5. It's almost comical that the online encyclopedia Wikipedia entry for Joey "Doves" Aiuppa, who took over as Outfit boss in 1971, says that in June 1975 he "allegedly conspired with Johnny 'Johnny Handsome' Roselli to kill Sam Giancana" but it simply shows "citation needed" for the claim. Similarly, the

Wikipedia entry for Sam Giancana lacks citations for the competing theories that we was killed by the CIA, Santo Trafficante, or Johnny Roselli, concluding without citation that "most investigators believe Aiuppa ordered the Giancana murder." https://en.wikipedia.org/wiki/Joseph_Aiuppa.

6. "When an angry, and politically fearful Mayor Daley declared "war on gangs" in 1969 he did not mean the Outfit, to whom he and the machine worked hand in . . . well . . . pocket. . . . "Organized crime" now meant black and Latino gangs, conveniently averting public attention from the much more powerful Outfit, who was in profitable cahoots with the machine and their police. In the years ahead, Chicago's Outfit would control Las Vegas and much of Hollywood through obedient Chicago-raised Jewish gangsters. . . . Outfit murders still were almost never solved by local officials. In fact, The Chicago Crime Commission . . . reported that of 33 mob confirmed slayings in the 1980s, only one was cleared [citations omitted]."

John M. Hagedorn, "A Genealogy of Gangs in Chicago: Bringing the State Back into Gang Research," paper presented at the Global Gangs Conference, Geneva, Switzerland, May 2009, http://gangresearch.net/Archives/hagedorn/articles/genealogyfinal.pdf.

15. OLD HAUNTS

1. Jeff Coen, "Hit Man's Son Takes Stand; Witness Backs Mobster's Brother," *Chicago Tribune Online*, July 25, 2007, accessed July 2, 2017, http://articles.chicagotribune.com/2007-07-25/news/0707241079_1_gambling-operation-nicholas-calabrese-chicago-outfit.

17. WHEN YOU GOT A JOB TO DO, BETTER DO IT WELL

1. A photograph of the doormat appears in the *Chicago Tribune* of June 21, 1975.

2. "Mob Silenced Giancana," *Chicago Sun-Times*, June 21, 1975, 1, accessed July 4, 2017. http://caponemaygofree.com/capone/index.php?option=com_joomgallery&func=detail&id=73&Itemid=43#joomimg. "Doorway to Death?," *High Point (N.C.) Enterprise*, June 21, 1975, 1.

3. Seth S. King, "Giancana, Gangster, Slain; Tied to C.I.A. Castro Plot," *New York Times*, June 21, 1975, 12.

4. The Oak Park police pronounced the investigation "a dead end." Norman Kempster, "Dead Mobster Had Interesting Friends, and Foes," *Montana Standard* (Butte), January 2, 1976, 4.

5. Bryce Nelson, "Mystery Still Shrouds Sam Giancana's Slaying," *Pittsburgh Press*, January 29, 1976, 17.

6. "Little Known about Murder of Sam Giancana," *Edwardsville (Ill.) Intelligencer,* December 30, 1975, 2.

18. THE PUZZLE PIECES

1. This was documented in a subsequent action by Giancana's daughters challenging a search warrant after Giancana's death: *People Ex Rel. Carey v. Covelli,* 61 Ill. 2d 394 (1975), 336 N.E.2d 759, https://law.justia.com/cases/illinois /supreme-court/1975/47714–6.html, accessed April 30, 2017.

2. *People Ex Rel. Carey v. Covelli.*

3. Ibid.

4. Jack Anderson, *Yuma (Ariz.) Daily Sun,* July 13, 1975, 4: "The word has been whispered around the underworld, according to our sources who have been reliable in the past, that Giancana was shot by a former girlfriend he had abused."

5. Weldon Whisler and John O'Brien, "Cops Watching Home Night Giancana Slain," *Chicago Sun-Times,* June 21, 1975, 5.

6. George Lardner Jr. and Caroline Rooney, "U.S. Says Crime Boss Cleared Dorfman Killing," *Washington Post,* January 3, 1986, accessed May 1, 2017, https://www.washingtonpost.com/archive/politics/1986/01/23/us-says-crime -boss-cleared-dorfman-killing/d737225f-1e38–4de9–872a-3df62ee2cff4/?utm _term=.e391b8b833e3.

7. Chuck Goudie, "ABC7 I-Team: Chicago Mobster Sam Giancana's 40-Year-Old Murder Still a Mystery," *ABC 7 Chicago Eyewitness News,* June 19, 2015, accessed April 30, 2017, http://abc7chicago.com/news/chicago-mobsters-40 -year-old-murder-still-a-mystery/795393/.

8. William Roemer, *Man against the Mob* (New York: Donald I. Fine, 1989). His book was the basis for Sugartime, an HBO movie about Giancana.

9. Antoinette Giancana and Tony C. Renner, *Mafia Princess: Growing Up in Sam Giancana's Family* (Morrow Press, 1984).

10. Goudie, "ABC7 I-Team."

11. Michael J. Corbitt, *Double Deal: The Inside Story of Murder, Unbridled Corruption, and the Cop who was a Mobster* (Avon Books, 2003), 194–97.

12. Corbitt, *Double Deal,* 196.

13. For a broad account of the Family Secrets trial see Jeff Coen, *Family Secrets: The Case That Crippled the Chicago Mob* (Chicago: Chicago Review Press, 2009).

14. Coen, *Family Secrets,* 17.

15. "FBI Accused of Killing Gangsters," *Palm Beach (Fla.) Post,* June 26, 1977, 5.

16. This kind of hit indicates the target's willingness to talk got him killed. "Through the mouth: a message job through the mouth to indicate that someone WAS a rat," The Godfather's Mafia Dictionary, http://www.performancetwo.com /mobspeak.htm. "Police view the method as a traditional underworld warning

to others who might be inclined to talk too much." Whisler and O'Brien, "Cops Watching Home Night Giancana Slain," 5.

17. William Brashler, "Death of a 'Godfather,'" *New York Magazine*, July 28, 1975, 32.

18. "Mob Suspected in Slaying of Chieftain with CIA Ties," *Arizona Republic* (Phoenix), June 21, 1975, 1, 5.

19. "Oak Park detectives said later that Mr. DiPersio's call for help did not come until 11:53 P.M. They assumed that Mr. DiPersio, who was once questioned about an earlier gang slaying, had first telephoned Mr. Giancana's two married daughters who live in the Chicago suburbs." Seth S. King, "Giancana, Gangster, Slain; Tied to C.I.A. Castro Plot," *New York Times*, June 21, 1975, 1.

20. "Report Covelli on Giancana Wedding List," *Chicago Tribune*, June 29, 1975, accessed June 12, 2017, http://archives.chicagotribune.com/1975/06/29 /page/12/article/report-covelli-on-giancana-wedding-list/index.html, accessed June 12, 2017.

21. William Safire, "Murder Most Foul," *New York Times*, December 22, 1975, 28; James Elsener and John O'Brien, "Carey to Subpoena Hoods at Party for Giancana," *Chicago Tribune*, June 22, 1975, 3.

22. Vincent L. Inserra, *C-1 and the Chicago Mob* (Xlibris, 2014). Accardo, English, and Blasi took the Fifth. Ibid.

23. Bryce Nelson, "Mystery Still Shrouds Sam Giancana's Slaying," *Pittsburgh Press*, January 29, 1976, 17.

24. "'Likely suspect" pegged in '75 Giancana slaying," *Chicago News Journal*, September 9, 1976, 66.

25. "Mafia Kingpin's Treasures," *Muncie (Ind.) Evening Press*, June 12, 1976, 8. Another auction was held in 2014; Jon Kass, "Pieces of Chicago Mob History up for Auction," *Chicago Tribune*, November 19, 2014, accessed June 12, 2017, http:// www.chicagotribune.com/news/columnists/kass/ct-kass-met-1119–20141119 -column.html.

26. Jay Gentile, "Gangster Tour Returns to Oak Park and River Forest," *Pioneer Press/Chicago Tribune*, June 19, 2015 accessed June 1, 2017, http://www. chicagotribune.com/suburbs/oak-park/lifestyles/ct-oak-go-gangster-tour-tl -0611–20150619-story.html.

27. Mike Robinson, "Widow: Hubby Drove Mercedes to His Death," *Northwest Herald* (Woodstock, Ill.), July 25, 2007, 4C.

28. Glenn Kessler, "Trying to Kill Fidel Castro," *Washington Post*, June 27, 2007, http://www.washingtonpost.com/wp-dyn/content/article/2007/06/26 /AR2007062601467.html, accessed June 12, 2017.

29. Nicholas Gage, "Mafia Said to Have Slain Rosselli Because of His Senate Testimony," *New York Times*, February 25, 1977, 1.

EPILOGUE: FROM THE MOB TO THE MINES

1. "Prosecutors blame mob boss James Marcello for the D'Andrea killing in one of the seemingly endless feuds that marked the Chicago Outfit, as the city's organized crime family calls itself, in the 1970s and 1980s." Mike Robinson, "Widow: Hubby Drove Mercedes to His Death," *Northwest Herald* (Woodstock, Ill.), July 25, 2007, 4C.

2. Ibid.

3. Mike Robinson, "Feds Indict 14 Reputed Mob Figures in Murders Stretching Back Decades," *Chicago Herald and Review,* April 25, 2005, accessed April 30, 2017, http://www.nwitimes.com/news/local/feds-indict-reputed-mob-figures-in-murders-stretching-back-decades/article_e56c78ad-7841–5290–9f9c-5f4c281525bf.html.

4. Mario's death is described in John O'Brien, "Drug Sale Suspect Slain in Suburb," *Chicago Tribune,* October 2, 1981, 3.

5. John O'Brien, "Mob Kingpin Tocco Convicted," *Chicago Tribune,* December 8, 1989, 29. "Tocco was indicted on federal charges in 1988 and fled overseas to Greece but was eventually captured by the FBI and convicted on multiple counts of racketeering. In a first for the Chicago Outfit, Tocco's wife, Betty, testified against her own husband, implicating him in several killings, including the brutal 1986 murders of Anthony Spilotro and his brother Michael." Lombardo, *Organized Crime in Chicago,* 184.

6. Toolan, "Prisoners Profit by Brush with Society."

INDEX

CHARLES HAGER is a native of West Virginia who first traveled to Chicago Heights at age nine with his Uncle Columbus. He moved there permanently as a young teen. Dubbed "Little Joe College" by Albert Tocco, he gradually worked his way from sweeping up his uncle's bar to a position of responsibility and trust as a friend of the Chicago Outfit. He left the Heights in 1975 and built a series of successful businesses in West Virginia and North Carolina. This is his first book.

DAVID T. MILLER is a writer and an editor based in Lexington, Kentucky.